D0773083

ATTENTION IN A SOCIAL WORLD

OXFORD SERIES IN SOCIAL COGNITION AND SOCIAL NEUROSCIENCE

Series Editor: RAN R. HASSIN

Editorial Board

MAHZARIN BANAJI
JOHN A. BARGH
JOHN GABRIELI
DAVID HAMILTON
ELIZABETH A. PHELPS
YAACOV TROPE

The New Unconscious
Edited by RAN R. HASSIN, JAMES S. ULEMAN, and JOHN A. BARGH

Oxford Handbook of Human Action
Edited by EZEQUIEL MORSELLA, JOHN A. BARGH, and PETER M. GOLLWITZER

**Social Neuroscience: Toward Understanding the Underpinnings
of the Social Mind**
Edited by ALEXANDER TODOROV, SUSAN T. FISKE, and DEBORAH PRENTICE

Self Control in Society, Mind, and Brain
Edited by RAN R. HASSIN, KEVIN N. OCHSNER, and YAACOV TROPE

Forthcoming:

Oxford Handbook of Social Neuroscience
Edited by JEAN DECETY and JOHN T. CACIOPPO

Beyond Pleasure and Pain
TORY E. HIGGINS

Attention in a Social World
MICHAEL I. POSNER

ATTENTION IN A
SOCIAL WORLD

Michael I. Posner

OXFORD
UNIVERSITY PRESS

OXFORD

UNIVERSITY PRESS

Oxford University Press, Inc., publishes works that further
Oxford University's objective of excellence
in research, scholarship, and education.

Oxford   New York
Auckland   Cape Town   Dar es Salaam   Hong Kong   Karachi
Kuala Lumpur   Madrid   Melbourne   Mexico City   Nairobi
New Delhi   Shanghai   Taipei   Toronto

With offices in
Argentina   Austria   Brazil   Chile   Czech Republic   France   Greece
Guatemala   Hungary   Italy   Japan   Poland   Portugal   Singapore
South   Korea   Switzerland   Thailand   Turkey   Ukraine   Vietnam

Copyright © 2012 by Michael I. Posner

Published by Oxford University Press, Inc.
198 Madison Avenue, New York, New York 10016
www.oup.com

Oxford is a registered trademark of Oxford University Press

All rights reserved. No part of this publication may be reproduced,
stored in a retrieval system, or transmitted, in any form or by any means,
electronic, mechanical, photocopying, recording, or otherwise,
without the prior permission of Oxford University Press.

Library of Congress Cataloging-in-Publication Data
Posner, Michael I.
Attention in a social world / Michael I. Posner.
p. cm.—(Oxford series in social cognition and social neuroscience)
Includes bibliographical references and index.
ISBN: 978-0-19-979121-7 (hardback : alk. paper)

1. Attention.   I. Title.

BF321.P67 2011
153.7′33—dc23

2011036758

3 5 7 9 8 6 4
Printed in the United States of America
on acid-free paper

PREFACE

In July of 2009, I received an e-mail from the board of Oxford Series in Social Cognition and Social Neuroscience asking me if I would be able to write a small volume on attention. I asked them if it would be appropriate to write what I thought a student of these topics might most need to know about attention rather than developing an overall review of the field of attention. They replied that it would be appropriate. I had a clear idea about what students interested in social cognition might need to know about attention and so the book was written very rapidly and a few months later I submitted a completed volume.

The completed volume was sent to Oxford for review Jan 2010. There were four extensive reviews, all by experts in attention. They found many things were missing, inappropriate, or redundant. All the reviews were from the perspective of neuroscience or cognitive neuroscience. Their primary perspective was accuracy and completeness not forging a link between attention and social neuroscience. One even suggested I simply rename the book *Attention*. I resisted all of these efforts although I did correct many things that were clear errors or even poorer writing than has eventually emerged. I still hope this book will deal with attention in a broad way that indicates how it might be applied to important social topics from education to clinical syndromes. The breadth of the treatment risks missing important issues within each of the senses of attention with which this book deals. However, it is most important that students know the various literatures involved and then they can follow up on the latest studies. Certainly many of the "facts" reported here may change with new research. Nonetheless, I hope the volume provides a rationale for connecting psychological measurement of individuals to brain networks and genes. The development of brain networks related to self-regulation is bound to remain a central topic for all who are interested in psychological issues. I was able to submit a revised version in March of 2011. After copyediting and adding this preface it is the book you are holding.

I would like to thank all of those whose efforts contributed to this volume, in particular the many colleagues and students whose studies are cited. I also thank Bob Rafal, Steve Hillyard, Yiyuan Tang, and the anonymous referees who managed to read some or all of the versions and provide often very detailed comments. I know I have not been able to fully implement all of their suggestions, but I appreciate their help. My colleague Prof. Mary Rothbart has been the major force in connecting brain networks to individual differences in development and her influence on this volume is very great. I am also grateful to Prof. David A. Washburn who is PI of NICHD grant HD 060563, which has provided support for the research described in this volume. I also appreciate the work of Oxford's editors including Catharine Carlin and Joan Bossert for trying to get the book done in a timely fashion.

I sincerely hope this small volume will be helpful for those hoping to do research in or make use of the findings of social cognition and social neuroscience.

Michael Posner
Eugene, Oregon
August 2011

CONTENTS

INTRODUCTION

The study of attention is central to psychology. When the goal was to separate psychology from physiology by building it upon subjective experience, this was done through the study of events accessible via introspection, which thus could be reported by the subject. Psychology was confined to our experience of the world as human beings and was separate from the study of the physical basis of mental events that were not conscious.

This separation no longer applies in the era of cognitive and social neuroscience. Imaging methods have broken down the distinction between psychology and physiology. This is all for the good, but it can also have some problematic consequences. Neuroscience seeks to understand brains, and the simpler the brain, the more fundamental the study. Thus, the human brain is not so often chosen for study, and when it is, often only the very simplest of situations are observed. In the field of attention, this has meant a concentration on light flashes, clicks, or other simple sensory input. This unfortunately leaves the impression that human attention is mostly about selecting sensory input, despite the fact that we obviously also attend to language, internal thoughts, dreams, and other human beings. This volume seeks to view attention in this larger social context, including our ability to voluntarily choose and act upon an object of thought.

Voluntary control of thought raises the specter of the homunculus, a little person inside the head who carries out higher mental processes and selects among response options (a model perhaps taken seriously centuries ago, but which now stands as a symbol of fallacious thinking about the mind). Rather than positing a little man, however, this volume is about the physical mechanisms by which conflicts are solved and responses emitted. Studying the mechanisms of self-regulation involves giving physical reality to what has been subjective (Posner & Rothbart, 2009).

The idea of reducing psychological concepts to their physical basis is an old theme in philosophical and scientific circles. The paradigm case for this kind of reduction is probably an understanding of "consciousness." Although a complete understanding of consciousness still seems remote, full reductionism is only one reason for seeking an understanding of psychological concepts at the level of neurons, molecules, and proteins. Even if full reduction remains only a distant or even impossible goal, some illumination of complex concepts, such as aspects of consciousness, is now possible.

One way of thinking about this issue is that the psychological concept of attention is to an understanding of consciousness as DNA is to an understanding of life (Posner, 1994; for another view see Koch & Tsuchiya, 2007). Even though DNA does not explain all the aspects of what it means to be living, no one doubts that knowledge of DNA leads to a much better scientific understanding of life. Similarly, consciousness is illuminated by understanding the networks of attention. Tellingly, the genetics of attention is now important in understanding the origin and physical basis of attentional networks (Green et al., 2008; Posner, Rothbart, & Sheese, 2007), providing an opportunity to examine the physical basis of complex psychological concepts such as self-regulation and their relationship to conscious control.

This volume reviews progress in understanding the physical basis of a complex psychological function. Consciousness can be divided into two topics: awareness of the world around us, and voluntary control of our own thoughts and behaviors. Although there has probably been more effort devoted to understanding conscious awareness, particularly of the visual world (Dennett, 2001; Koch & Tsuchaya, 2007), this volume concentrates on aspects of voluntary control, particularly as they arise early in life as a result of infant socialization. This aspect of voluntary control is often called self-regulation. Every parent is aware of the remarkable transformation from infancy to childhood as children develop the ability to regulate their emotions and to persist in working toward goals in the face of distractions. Even though self-regulation does not deal with all aspects of volition—and even fewer aspects of consciousness—it is of sufficient complexity and centrality to serve as a model system for illuminating a psychological concept by examining its physical basis. The results of our examination of volition also cast some light on self-control as a central aspect of adult life and even on aspects of awareness.

THE ROAD TO OUR PRESENT KNOWLEDGE

Considerable progress along these avenues of inquiry was made in the years and decades following World War II. A quick review of some key developments along the way will provide a useful overview of the basis for this book.

In 1949, Hebb argued that all stimuli have two effects. One of these, following the studies of Moruzzi and Magoun (1949), involved the reticular activating system and worked to keep the cortex tuned during the waking state, whereas the other used the great sensory pathways and provided information about the nature of the stimulating event.

Another milestone was Cherry's work. In 1953, he initiated an epic series of experiments designed to examine how subjects selected stimuli that were presented simultaneously. A major observation was that rapid presentation of pairs of digits, one to each ear, led subjects to recall all digits presented to the right ear first, followed by all presented to the left ear. Broadbent (1958) summarized these and other results by suggesting that a peripheral short-term memory system buffers sensory input prior to a filter, which selects a channel of entry (in this case an ear) and sends information to a limited-capacity perceptual system. My reading of Broadbent's book when I first entered graduate school was a central impetus to my choosing to work on attention.

A second line of attention research that emerged from studies conducted during World War II involved the study of sustained attention during vigilance tasks (Mackworth & Mackworth, 1956). During continuous tasks, subjects tended to miss more signals as the task continued. Sometimes these were called blocks when subjects seemed to have tuned out, and changes in EEG suggested an increase in a sleep-like state.

One of the big developments of the 1960s involved the ability to average electrical signals from the scalp to develop the event-related potential (ERP), as a series of electrical events time-locked to the presentation of the stimulus. This technique was applied to the study of attention. Sutton et al. (1965) reported that surprising or unexpected cognitive events, of the type that might be closely inspected, produced a strong positive wave in the scalp potential called the P300. This component continues to play an important role in attention research (Donchin & Cohen, 1967; Rugg & Coles, 1995).

At about the same time, Walter reported that the brain produced a marked DC shift during the period following a warning signal and prior to a target. Walter called this the contingent negative variation (CNV) and viewed it as a sign that alerting was taking place (Walter et al., 1964). Reaction time improved markedly over the first 500 milliseconds following the warning, and often errors increased with the warning interval, producing a tradeoff between speed and accuracy. This finding suggested that warning effects did not improve the accrual of information but instead made the subject faster to attend to the input, thus speeding the response (Posner, 1978).

Then, in 1968, Hubel and Wiesel used microelectrodes to probe the structure of the visual system. Before this method could be applied to attention, however, it was necessary to adapt the microelectrode technique to alert animals. This was accomplished in the early 1970s and applied by Mountcastle (1978) and Wurtz, Goldberg, and Robinson (1980) to examine mechanisms of visual attention in the superior colliculus and parietal lobe. Their findings suggested the importance of both of these areas to a shift of visual attention. It had been known for many years that patients with lesions of the right parietal lobe could suffer from a profound neglect of space opposite the lesion. The findings of "attention-related cells" in the posterior parietal lobe of alert monkeys suggested that these cells might be responsible for the clinical syndrome of neglect.

An impressive result from the microelectrode work was that the time course of parietal cell activity seemed to follow a visual stimulus by 80 to 100 milliseconds. Beginning in the 1970s, Hillyard (e.g., van Voorhis & Hillyard, 1978) and other investigators explored the use of scalp electrodes to examine time differences in neural activity between attended and unattended visual locations. They found that early parts of the visual ERP showed changes due to attention starting at about 100 milliseconds after input. These findings showed likely convergence of the latency of psychological processes as measured by ERPs in human subjects and cellular processes in alert monkeys. These results were an important development for mental chronometry (i.e., the study of the time course of information processing in the human brain) because they suggested that scalp recordings could accurately reflect the underlying temporal structure of brain activity.

In 1980, I studied the use of a cue in an otherwise empty visual field as a way of moving attention to a target (Posner, 1980). Electrodes near the eyes were used to ensure no eye movement. Because only one response was required, there was no way to prepare the response differently depending on the cue. This made it clear that whatever changes were induced by the cue were covert and not due to motor adjustment of the eyes or hand.

It was found that covert shifts could enhance the speed of responding to the target even in a nearly empty field. Within half a second, one could shift attention to a visual event and, when it indicated a likely target at another location, move attention to enhance processing at the new location. It was shown (Shulman, Remington, & McClean, 1979) that response times to probes at intermediate locations were enhanced at intermediate times as though attention actually moved through space. It was also shown to be possible to prepare to move the eyes to one direction while moving attention covertly in the opposite direction (Posner, 1980). Whether attention moves through the intermediate space, and how free covert attention is from the eye movement systems, are still disputed matters (LaBerge, 1995; Rizzolatti et al., 1987). Chapter 3 revisits these issues with new neuroimaging and cellular recording studies.

At the time, it was also hard to understand how a movement of attention could possibly be executed by neurons. Subsequently, it was shown that the population vector of a set of neurons in the motor system of a monkey could carry out what would appear behaviorally as a mental rotation (Georgopoulos et al., 1989). After that finding, a covert shift of attention did not seem too far-fetched.

It had been reported that patients with lesions of the parietal lobe could make same-different judgments concerning objects that they were unable to report consciously (Volpe, LeDoux, & Gazzaniga, 1979). It was also possible to follow this result in more analytic cognitive studies. What did a right parietal lesion do that made access to material on the left side of space difficult or impossible for consciousness and yet still allowed the information to be available for other judgments?

This puzzle was partially answered by the systematic study of patients with lesions in various locations in the parietal lobe, the pulvinar, and the colliculus. Patients with these lesions all tended to show neglect of the side of space opposite the lesion. But in a detailed cognitive analysis, it became clear that their deficits were in different specific mental operations involved in shifting attention (Posner, 1988). These studies supported a limited form of brain localization. The hypothesis was that different brain areas executed individual mental operations or computations, such as disengaging from the current focus of attention (parietal lobe), moving or changing the focus of attention (colliculus), and engaging the subsequent target (pulvinar). If this hypothesis were correct, it might explain why Lashley thought the whole brain was involved in mental tasks. Perhaps it's not the whole brain's activity, but instead a widely dispersed network of quite localized neural areas.

In the late 1980s, the Washington University School of Medicine was developing a center for neuroimaging using positron emission tomography (PET). The center was led by Marc Raichle. These studies helped establish neuroimaging as a means of exploring brain activity during cognitive functions in general and attention in particular (Posner & Raichle, 1994, 1998). In general, these studies showed that most cognitive tasks, including those that are designed to explore mechanisms of attention, have activated a small number of widely scattered neural areas. Some people have argued that these areas are specific for such domains of function as language, face perception, or episodic memory (Kanwisher & Duncan, 2004). In the area of attention, it has been more frequent to consider the common mental operations or computations carried out by a particular area (Corbetta & Shulman, 2002; Posner, 2004). These two ideas are not mutually exclusive; it is certainly possible to talk about the areas that are involved in language and at the same time maintain that these areas carry out different computations within that domain.

The findings from neuroimaging that cognitive tasks involve a number of different anatomical areas led to an emphasis on tracing the time dynamics of these areas during tasks involving attention. Because shifts of attention can be so rapid, it is difficult to follow them with hemodynamic imaging. To fill this role, algorithms were developed (Scherg & Berg, 1993) to relate the scalp distribution recorded from high-density electrical or magnetic sensors on or near the skull to brain areas active during hemodynamic imaging (see Dale et al., 2000, for a review). In some areas of attention, there has been extensive validation of these algorithms (Heinze et al., 1994), and they allow precise data on the sequence of activations during the selection of visual stimuli (see Hillyard, Di Russo, & Martinez, 2004, for a review). The combination of spatial localization with hemodynamic imaging and temporal precisions from electrical or magnetic recording has provided an approach to revealing the dynamic operations of the networks underlying attention.

At the turn of the century, the overall sequence of the human genome was reported (Venter et al., 2001). Although humans have a common genome, there are differences among individuals in many genes (polymorphisms). These differences make it possible to examine particular genes related to individual differences in behavior and brain activity (Goldberg & Weinberger, 2004; Mattay & Goldberg, 2004).

GOALS OF THIS VOLUME

The present volume is largely a personal statement. It does not seek to review all studies or controversies in the field, but rather to lay out, across seven chapters, one approach to understanding the attention system of the human brain and its consequences for our development in a social world.

Chapter 1 sets the stage by outlining the brain network approach to the analysis of attention. The importance of brain networks is supported by a vast array of results from neuroimaging studies, which rely on a tool kit of methods needed to trace brain networks; this chapter reviews many of those methods.

Chapters 2 to 4 define three brain networks associated with the functions of attention. These networks have a certain degree of independence, so they can profitably be discussed in separate chapters; nonetheless, in life these networks operate together to define the brain's attention system. Chapter 2 deals with obtaining and maintaining the alert state, Chapter 3 with orienting to sensory events, and Chapter 4 with a frontal network involved in voluntary control.

Chapter 5 deals specifically with the evolutionary and developmental history of these attention networks, including their relationship to issues of socialization during development. Chapter 6 provides details on how attention operates in clinics and schools, and the ability of attention to illuminate topics in cognitive and social neuroscience. Finally, Chapter 7 provides a summary of what has been reviewed in this volume.

ATTENTION IN A SOCIAL WORLD

The Attention System of the Human Brain

Attention is relatively easy to define subjectively, as in the classical definition by the great American psychologist and philosopher William James, who said, "Everyone knows what attention is. It is the taking possession of the mind in clear and vivid form of one out of what seem several simultaneous objects or trains of thought" (1890).

However, this subjective definition does not provide hints that might lead to an understanding of attentional development, self-regulation, or individual or cultural differences. Alexander Luria (1973), the famous Russian neuropsychologist, distinguished between an automatic attention system for orienting to sensory events (Sokolov, 1958) and a higher-level attention system identified by Vygotsky (1934), who believed that—unlike the orienting system—it was largely social in origin rather than biological.

THE BRAIN NETWORK APPROACH

A major theme of this volume is that it is now possible to view attention much more concretely as an organ system, with its own functional anatomy and its own evolution and development. This system can be further broken down into at least three constituent networks. According to Webster's dictionary, "An organ system may be defined as differentiated structures in animals and plants made up of various cell and tissues and adapted for the performance of some specific function and grouped with other structures into a system."

This view of attention as an organ system aids in answering many perplexing issues raised in cognitive psychology, psychiatry, and neurology. Neuroimaging studies have systemically shown that a wide variety of cognitive tasks can be seen as activating a distributed set of neural areas, many of which can be identified with specific mental operations (Posner & Raichle, 1994, 1998). Perhaps the areas of activation identified in studies of attention have been more consistent than in any other cognitive system. We can view attention as involving specialized networks to carry out functions, such as achieving and maintaining the alert state, orienting to sensory events, and controlling thoughts and feelings. In Chapters 4 and 5, we trace the origins of the higher-level system that Vygotsky described and show how genes and environment together shape its development.

The idea of neural networks as the basic units underlying thought goes back to the work of the Canadian neuropsychologist D.O. Hebb and his 1949 book *The Organization of Behavior*. At the time Hebb wrote his monograph, relatively little was known about how the structure and organization of the central nervous system contributed to the functions observed in psychological studies. This led Hebb to talk in terms of the conceptual nervous system and ideas about its structure that might be imagined or inferred from psychological studies. The methods available to Hebb, mostly animal research and human behavioral experiments, were not sufficient to provide empirical data for linking his conceptual nervous system to real events in the human brain. This methodology has now been provided by neuroimaging. While Hebb also recognized the importance of studying individual differences in intelligence and affect, there were also no methods for exploring the specific genes that are an important source of these differences. The human genome project has provided new methods for exploring this issue.

In Hebb's time, the idea of a network (cell assembly or phase sequence) was a rather vague verbal abstraction that did not allow for models that could produce specific predictions. Due to rapid advances in cellular biology (Bullock, Bennett, Johnston, Josephson, Marder, & Fields, 2005) and in the mathematics of multilevel networks, this too has changed (Rumelhart & McClelland, 1986). Although early versions of these networks were inspired by simple views of neurons as all-or-none elements, more recent versions (O'Reilly & Munakata, 2000) have begun to use the details of neuroanatomy and cellular structure as provided by imaging and cellular studies to develop networks that take more realistic advantage of the structure of the human brain. Hebb's basic idea, together with new methodological tools and new disciplines (e.g., cognitive, affective, and social neuroscience), all based on network views, give abundant evidence of the value of employing the converging operations strategy.

Hebb's book was immediately recognized as providing the potential for an integrated psychology. One reviewer (Attneave, 1950, p. 633) wrote:

I believe *The Organization of Behavior* to be the most important contribution to psychological theory in recent years. Unlike those of his contemporaries who are less interested in psychology than in some restricted aspect thereof to which their principles confine them, Hebb has made a noteworthy attempt to take the experimentally determined facts of behavior, as they are, and account for them in terms of events within the central nervous system.

The idea of a synapse that could be modified by experience, the Hebb synapse, has had wide currency in neuroscience (see Milner, 2003; Kolb, 2003; Sejnowski, 2003). For psychology and social neuroscience, the most important basic idea that Hebb presented was the cell assembly theory outlined in Chapters 4 and 5 of his book (see Goddard, 1980). Hebb argued that every psychological event, sensation, expectation, emotion, or thought is represented by the flow of activity in a set of interconnected neurons. Learning occurs by a change in synaptic strength when a synapse conducts excitation at the same time the postsynaptic neuron discharges. This provided a basis for the modification of synapses and showed how neural networks might be organized under the influence of specific experiences. The Hebb synapse plays a central role in modern neuroscience. There are important new developments in the study of synapses and in the discovery of other influences among neurons and between neurons and other brain cells (Bullock et al., 2005). These developments have reduced the gap between networks revealed in imaging studies and the complex intercellular activity in cell assemblies. In particular, they show that learning may reflect different mechanisms that influence these interactions at many time scales and may be modified by aspects of the organism's overall state.

Hebb also introduced the concept of the phase sequence involved in the coordination of multiple cell assemblies. He recognized the importance of the temporal correspondence between assemblies. In recent years, these ideas have been supported by studies showing that synchronization of neural activity in different brain areas may be critical to the detection of stimuli (Womelsdorf, Fries, Mitra, & Desimone, 2006) and for transfer of information between remote areas (Nikolaev, Ivanitsky, Ivanitsky, Abdullaev, & Posner, 2001; Womelsdorf et al., 2007). It has also been possible to see that learning can influence the efficiency of white matter connections between brain areas (Tang et al., 2010).

NEW TOOLS

Several major late-20th-century developments offer improved prospects for the ideas introduced by Hebb. Notably, thanks to work on the computational properties of neural networks (i.e., Rumelhart & McClelland, 1986; O'Reilly & Munakata, 2000), it is possible to develop more detailed theories integrating information from physiological, cognitive, and behavioral studies. Next, we review tools designed to understand brain activation and connectivity.

Activation

Efforts to image the living human brain are ancient but had met with little success until the modern era began with mathematical algorithms that allowed X-rays to be combined to produce a picture of the brain's structure: computerized tomography or CT scans. However, the images most needed for understanding the brain during the performance of everyday tasks were pictures of its function, not its structure. These efforts began with the use of radionucleotides that emit photons when in contact with matter.

Counts of the frequency of these emissions were used to construct maps of changes in blood flow at various locations in the brain, which provided information on brain activity during task performance. The major methods used to develop these maps were single photon emission computerized tomography (SPECT) and positron emission tomography (PET) (for an extensive history of this field, see Savoy, 2001).

It was known from animal studies that the activity of brain cells (neurons) was related to increased blood flow in the region of the activity. Using measures of cerebral blood flow, it was possible to show which portions of the brain were active. This mapping method was first employed using tasks like reading or listening to music to show that much of the brain, but not the entire brain, exhibited increased blood flow (Lassen, Ingvar, & Skinhoj, 1978). In an important early study, tasks including navigation, reading, and imaging were compared to show clear regional distribution of brain activity that differed between tasks (Roland & Friberg, 1985). Tasks such as reading and visual imagery had been analyzed by cognitive psychologists and divided into component operations or in computer language subroutines that were sufficient to perform the task (Kosslyn, 1980; Posner & Raichle, 1994). An important step toward making brain maps useful in psychology and education was taken with the development of a strategy for relating these component operations to brain areas.

The initial step in this direction used PET and examined activation patterns when reading individual nouns (Petersen, Fox, Posner, et al., 1987). In different blocks of trials, subjects either (1) watched a fixation point while nothing occurred, (2) listened or watched words passively, (3) repeated each word aloud, or (4) generated the use of each word. By subtracting each task from the next one, it was possible to isolate mental operations. When subjects read words aloud, the major activity was in motor areas and in the left anterior insula, but when they generated the use of a word as a noun, they activated left anterior frontal, cingulate, and cerebellar areas as well as a posterior temporal parietal area. The highly automated task of reading produced one set of activated areas, whereas when a novel association was required, a different set of areas was activated. During the naming of novel associations, the anterior cingulate is involved in attention to the task, while the left frontal area holds the stimulus in mind as activation in the posterior areas (Wernicke's area) produces the associated meaning. If the same list of words was repeated and participants made the same association, the strength of the activations related to the novel association decreased, and the set of activations became similar to reading the word aloud (Raichle, Fiez, Videen, et al., 1994). A few minutes of learning had automated the associations: they were made more reliably and faster so that each association was as directly connected to the visual word as it was in reading the word itself. These findings supported the isolation of mental operations and showed how well they adapted to learning.

A major development in 1990 was the use of magnetic resonance to measure localized changes in blood oxygen as a means of mapping brain activity noninvasively (Ogawa, Lee, Kay, et al., 1990). This technology, functional magnetic resonance imaging (fMRI), was not only able to reveal much more localized activity than PET, it had two other features very important for cognitive and educational work. First, it did not use any radioactivity, so any given subject could be repeatedly scanned, making it possible to map individual differences in brain activity and allowing its use with children. Second, it became possible to combine trials of different types within the same block of trials, so that participants could not develop a special strategy for each block of trials.

Much subsequent work has confirmed and elaborated the role of different brain areas in language production and understanding, particularly with respect to the skill of reading. Two important posterior brain areas, the left fusiform gyrus and the left temporal parietal lobe, operate automatically in the skilled reader. The left fusiform gyrus, often called the visual word form area (McCandliss, Cohen, & Dehaene, 2003), seems to be involved in chunking visual letters into a unit and appears to be of special importance in languages that are irregular in pronunciation. Although there has been dispute about this area (Price, 2003), most studies have found it to respond to groups of letters that could be pronounced, rather than to familiar words only. The activation of the left temporal parietal lobe is closer to the auditory system and appears to represent the sound of the visual word. These two areas operate automatically in skilled readers of English; they do not seem to work well in children who are having unusual difficulty learning to read.

The two posterior areas operate together with areas involved in effort or attention to the printed word and with grasping both the meaning of lexical items and of sentences and longer passages. The anterior cingulate gyrus is a major structure in the executive attention system and is important for regulating other brain networks, including those involved in reading. It operates in conjunction with a left lateral frontal area to hold in mind words while lexical meanings are retrieved from Wernicke's area and from the highly distributed areas that deal with meaning. Understanding the connotation of a word may involve information stored in sensory and motor areas as well as in Wernicke's area.

Use of fMRI has allowed the study of many brain networks related not only to cognitive processes such as reading, listening, imaging, and so on, but also to emotional, social, and personality-related processes. A partial list of these networks is shown in Table 1.1.

Table 1.1 SOME OF THE TOPICS IN PSYCHOLOGY FOR WHICH
UNDERLYING BRAIN NETWORKS HAVE BEEN EXAMINED*

Function	Selected Reference
Arithmetic	Dehaene (1997, Fig. 8.5)
Autobiographical Memory	Fink et al. (1996)
Fear	Ochsner et al. (2006)
Faces	Haxby (2004)
Music	Levitin (2006)
Object Perception	Grill-Spector (2004)
Reading and Listening	Posner & Raichle (1994)
Reward	Knutson et al. (2003)
Self Reference	Johnson et al. (2005)
Spatial Navigation	Shelton & Gabrieli (2002)
Working Memory	Smith et al. (1998)
	Ungerleider et al. (1998)

*One or two illustrative references are cited. They are not meant to be comprehensive.

Some (e.g., Utall, 2001) have argued that knowing where in the brain something happens is not very useful for understanding higher cognitive processes. However, imaging studies have gone well beyond simple localization to provide sets of neural areas that form networks. Brain networks in turn provided the impetus for examining how genes and experience build networks. Moreover, localization efforts with imaging methods quickly produced other techniques for probing the time courses and detailed computations carried out by these networks.

Connectivity

Neural areas found active in studies of functional anatomy must be orchestrated in carrying out any real task. One approach to studying this connectivity uses fMRI to study the time course of activity and the correlations between active areas. Below we illustrate these methods by primarily considering the connectivity of the anterior cingulate during tasks that involve attention. The anterior cingulate is active during the reading and listening tasks described in the last section. This area of the brain has large-scale connectivity to many other brain areas and is ideally situated to exercise executive control over other brain networks (Posner & Fan, 2008).

The executive attention network involves the ability to resolve conflict among the many active brain networks competing for the control of behavior. The anterior cingulate is part of a network that includes other important brain areas. According to Bush, Luu, and Posner (2000), an analysis of a number of conflict tasks shows that the more dorsal part of the anterior cingulate is involved in the regulation of cognitive tasks, while the more ventral part of the cingulate is involved in regulation of emotion. The dorsal part of the anterior cingulate has strong connections to frontal and parietal areas involved in cognitive processes. A much finer analysis of sub-areas of the anterior cingulate confirms the distinction between the ventral emotional and dorsal cognitive portions (Beckman, Johansen-Berg, & Rushworth, 2009).

During task performance, the anterior cingulate establishes contact with brain areas involved in processing information.

In one study, for example, participants selected either visual or auditory information. During the selection of visual information, the dorsal cingulate showed correlation with visual brain areas; these correlations switched to auditory areas when auditory information was chosen (Crottaz-Herbette & Mennon, 2006). When participants processed emotional information, the more ventral parts of the cingulate were active and connected to limbic areas such as the amygdala related to the emotion (Etkin, Egner, Peraza, et al., 2006).

It is also possible to apply dynamic casual modeling (DCM) to study the interaction among brain regions (Friston, Harrison, & Penny, 2003; Penny, Stephan, Mechelli, & Friston, 2004). This method examines which brain area sends information to which other brain areas. For example, we can investigate whether the connection between the anterior cingulate and the limbic system represents the influence of the ACC on the limbic area, a mutual connection, or primarily a limbic influence on the ACC.

Another approach to the measurement of connectivity involves the measurement of fiber tracts that connect neural areas by use of diffusion tensor imaging (DTI), which noninvasively images the white matter connections between brain areas. By following the diffusion of water molecules along particular paths due to the presence of myelinated fibers (Conturo, Lori, Cull, et al., 1999), it allows tracing of fiber pathways during different stages of human development and provides a way to examine the anatomical connections present in the brain

Because fMRI is noninvasive, it is possible to use multiple scans to examine changes that occur with learning and development (Kelly & Garavan, 2005). This is obviously an important tool for the study of development and learning. It is common for learning on a task to decrease the number and size of brain activations.

The rate of these changes may vary from milliseconds to years, depending on what is being learned. Connectivity of the network can also be enhanced by practice (McNamara, Tegenthoff, Hubert, et al., 2007; Tang et al 2010). Studies of changes in connectivity through the course of development show that local connections are dominant in children and longer connections are more prominent in adults (Fair et al., 2009). Developmental changes are often accompanied by reduced number and size of activations, just as is found for practice in a given task. More information on the effects of development and learning on brain activity will be presented in Chapter 5.

Event-related Potentials

Because of the relatively long delays between input and the peak fMRI signal, small time differences may be hard to detect. Another approach to the examination of temporal connections between brain areas is based on electrical or magnetic signals. These signals can give higher temporal resolution and can be combined with MRI to improve their spatial localization.

By measuring electrical (EEG) and magnetic (MEG) signals outside the skull, the time course of activation of different brain areas localized by fMRI can be measured (Dale et al., 2000). When a signal is presented many times, the electrical or magnetic activity can be averaged to form an event-related potential indicating the activity following each few milliseconds after presentation. For example, Dehaene (1996) used electrical recording from scalp electrodes to map out the time course of mental activity involved in determining whether a visual digit was above or below 5. He averaged brain electrical activity (event-related potential) following the presentation of a single digit that was to be classified as above or below 5. The first 100 milliseconds involved activity in the visual system. When the input was an Arabic digit, both hemispheres were active, but when it was a spelled digit (e.g., six), activity was found in the visual word form system. In the next 100 milliseconds, differences were found between digits either close to five (e.g., four or six) or from those further from five (e.g., two or nine). This difference was in electrodes over the parietal brain areas now known to be involved in representing the number line. Before output, there was activity in motor areas; following a trial in which the person made an error, there was an error-related negativity in electrodes over the frontal midline, localized to the anterior cingulate. Although recognition of the quantity of a digit is a very elementary aspect of numeracy, training in the appreciation of the value of a number has been shown to be an important contributor to success in elementary school arithmetic (Griffin, Case, & Siegler, 1995).

The complex electrical signal coming from scalp electrodes can be decomposed into sine and cosine waves by Fourier analysis. There is a great deal of interest in the functions of oscillations both in changes of brain state and in integrating brain activity in different brain systems. During deep sleep, slow waves predominate, and in the awake resting state, created by closing the eyes, alpha frequency (about 10 Hz) occurs, particularly over posterior electrodes. Following a self-detected error made in response to a task, there is activity in the theta region (3 Hz; Berger, Tzur, & Posner, 2006). It has been hypothesized that high-frequency gamma activity (40 Hz) is important in order to tie together distant brain regions that are analyzing a single object (Womelsdorf, et al., 2007).

Electrical recordings are sufficiently noninvasive to use with young children. This can make them useful for understanding what happens in the brain during infancy. Infants come into the world with the capability of discriminating among the units of language (phonemes) in all of the world's languages. For example, if one phoneme is sounded over and over again (e.g., *ba*) so that its novelty effects are reduced, a recovery occurs when a different phoneme is heard (e.g., *da*). Thus, the infant exhibits an auditory system capable of learning the phonemes to which it will be exposed. Moreover, in the period between 6 and 10 months, there is a considerable shaping of this phonemic structure (Kuhl, 2000). Those sounds to which the infant is exposed tend to solidify and form a unit, while the ability to discriminate unfamiliar sound units begins to disappear. Studies have shown that infants raised in English-speaking homes can maintain their ability to discriminate phonemes in Mandarin Chinese, for example, if exposed to a speaker of those sounds during this period (Kuhl, Tsao, & Liu, 2003). During this period, phonemes from the native language are also facilitated (Kuhl, Stevens, Hyashi, et al., 2006). Unfortunately, learning did not occur when the exposure was to a video rather than to an actual person. Current research is attempting to find the most important aspects of these early social interactions in the hope of being able to determine whether an electronic media presentation incorporating them could be designed. Observation of the tutor in these studies shows the elaborate methods that are used to maintain the interest of the infant. We simply do not know if an understanding of these methods may allow them to be duplicated by a nonsocial computer-based or robotic system. However, these findings and others like them show that the infant's auditory system is being trained by the speech patterns of its language community.

Experiments with infants have also shown that the effectiveness of this training can be measured by changes in scalp-recorded event-related potentials following a change from a frequent to an infrequent phoneme (Guttorm, Leppanen, Poikkeus, et al., 2005; Molfese, 2000). The brain shows its discrimination between the two by responding differently when the novel phoneme occurs. Brain activity can thus reveal whether or not the infant is making the discrimination between phonemes. This electrical difference can be used as a measure of the efficiency of the brain in making the discrimination. Using this method, we can examine the effectiveness of caregivers in establishing the phonemic structure of their native language and of additional languages they might desire to teach. It is also possible to predict later difficulties in spoken language and in reading from these recordings (Guttorm, et al., 2005; Molfese, 2000), although it is still unknown exactly how accurate these predictions can be. These methods make it possible to check for the development of a strong phonemic structure by use of electrical recording in early life, just as brain stem event-related potentials to sounds are widely used now to allow early detection of hearing deficits in infants.

The activation of brain networks does not mean that all parts of the network are needed to carry out the task. Traditionally, effects of brain lesions have been a primary way to indicate brain areas that, when lost, will prevent a person from carrying out certain tasks. For example, damage to areas of the right parietal lobe can lead to neglect of the left side of space in multiple sensory systems.

The high anatomical resolution of modern imaging techniques has greatly aided the study of brain lesions. Methods have been developed for superimposing the lesions of individual patients in a common space so that the areas of damage common to patients are revealed. In some cases, this has led to human lesion analysis, which is as precise as would be obtained from producing lesions in an animal model (Friedrich, Egly, Rafal, & Beck, 1998).

A good example of the use of lesion data in conjunction with imaging is a study of a patient who, after a stroke, was unable to read words when they were presented to the left of where he was currently looking (fixation) but could read them fluently when presented to the right of fixation (Cohen, Henry, Dehaene, et al., 2004). Imaging showed that there was interruption of the fibers that conducted information to the visual word form area from the right hemisphere occipital lobe. When words were presented to the left of fixation (i.e., directly to the right hemisphere), the patient could only sound them out letter by letter. However, he clearly maintained all the reading skills, as evidenced by his fluent performance with words presented to the right visual field (i.e., directly to the left hemisphere) so that they did reach the visual word form area. This study shows clearly that the visual word form area is a necessary condition for fluent reading.

It is now possible to use brief magnetic pulses applied to the scalp overlying the brain area of interest using transcortical magnetic stimulation (TMS) to disrupt parts of the network at particular times to observe its influences on task performance. One striking example of this technology shows that the visual system is involved when reading Braille. When TMS was applied to the visual cortex, Braille readers had a specific problem in reading words, suggesting that the visual system was used to handle spatial aspects of the tactile input in Braille (Pascale-Leone & Hamilton, 2001).

Lesion data can be used to confirm and extend theories arising from imaging techniques. Although researchers are not usually confronted with patients with specific brain lesions due to stroke, findings from these patients can often illuminate specific learning difficulty, dyslexia, or dyscalculia (math disability) that arise in development.

Most imaging studies have been concerned with anatomical issues. Several functions of attention have been shown to involve specific anatomical areas that carry out important functions. However, imaging can also be used to probe neural networks that underlie all aspects of human thought, feelings, and behavior (Posner & Rothbart, 2007). Networks have been studied in all the topics shown in Table 1.1. The full meanings of imaging for (a) viewing brain networks, (b) examining their computation in real time, (c) exploring how they are assembled in development, and (d) revealing their plasticity following physical damage or training are common themes in research that is just beginning to reach its potential.

Another important development, mapping of the human genome (Venter et al., 2001), offers the potential for an increased understanding of the biological basis for individual differences in temperament, personality, etc. Many genes exhibit a number of relatively high-frequency variants (polymorphisms) that can code for different physical configurations. These in turn can alter the efficiency of a network. For example, different forms (alleles) of genes forming dopamine receptors can lead to different efficiencies in binding to dopamine and thus differences in underlying neural networks. In a number of cases, it has been possible to relate these genetic differences to individual performance in tasks involving a brain network (see Green et al., 2008, for a review). Genetics-based research also provides an important approach to the development of characteristics of neural networks common to all members of the species.

Any approach based on neural networks raises the issue of crude reductionism. Many agree that all human behavior must ultimately be traceable to brain activity, but correctly argue for the importance of cognitive experiments, behavioral observations, and self-reporting as important elements of psychological science. This volume tries to show how important such methods are, and how they can be integrated within a brain network framework.

Imaging Attention Networks

Functional neuroimaging has allowed many cognitive tasks to be analyzed in terms of the brain areas they activate, and studies of attention have been among those most often examined in this way (Corbetta & Shulman, 2002; Driver, Eimer, & Macaluso, 2004; Posner & Fan, 2008). Although there have been many functional distinctions made in the history of attention research (e.g., Kahneman, 1973), including vigilance, inhibitory control, internalized control, sustained attention, selective attention, and visual search, imaging data have supported the presence of three networks related to different aspects of attention (Fan et al., 2005). These networks carry out the functions of alerting, orienting, and executive attention (Posner & Fan, 2008). Although we do not know if these three networks will include all possible concepts related to attention, it seems likely that, alone or in combination, they do incorporate most or all of the various concepts of attention that have arisen. For example, sustained attention seems to involve maintaining the alert state, plus either orienting or executive control, depending on whether the information is sensory or in memory. Inhibitory control appears to be a part of the executive system that resolves conflict by reducing the effective activation in other networks. Of course, it is always possible that new data will support other attention networks. A summary of the anatomy and transmitters involved in the three networks is shown in Table 1.2.

Table 1.2 BRAIN AREAS AND NEUROMODULATORS INVOLVED
IN ATTENTION NETWORKS

FUNCTION	STRUCTURES	MODULATOR
Alert	Locus Coeruleus Right frontal and parietal cortex	Norepinephrine
Orient	Superior parietal Temporal parietal junction Frontal eye fields Superior colliculus	Acetylcholine
Executive attention	Anterior Cingulate Anterior Insula Prefrontal Basal Ganglia	Dopamine

Alerting is defined as achieving and maintaining a state of high sensitivity to incoming stimuli; *orienting* is the selection of information from sensory input; and *executive attention* involves mechanisms for monitoring and resolving conflict among thoughts, feelings, and responses.

The alerting system has been associated especially with the Locus Coeruleus of the brainstem and cingulate areas, as well as frontal and parietal regions of the cortex (Fan et al., 2005). A particularly effective way to vary alertness has been to use warning signals prior to targets. This produces a rapid phasic change in alertness. The influence of warning signals on the level of alertness is thought to be due to modulation of neural activity by the neurotransmitter norepinepherine (Marrocco & Davidson, 1998). Tonic alertness may be viewed as a brain state that fluctuates according to the time of day, fatigue, boredom, and other factors.

Orienting involves aligning attention with a source of sensory signals. This may be overt, as when eye movements accompany movements of attention, or it may occur covertly, without any eye movement. It is important to distinguish the brain system that is the source of attentional influences (sources) from the areas at which attention may have an effect (site). The sites at which attention may have an influence include all primary sensory and motor systems and many other brain areas. However, the source of these influences arises in a common orienting that is the source of the attention effect irrespective of the sensory system involved. This system includes the superior parietal lobe, temporal parietal junction, and frontal eye fields (Corbetta & Shulman, 2002). Lesion data have suggested that subcortical areas, including the superior colliculus and pulvinar, are also involved (Posner & Fan, 2008). Orienting can be manipulated by presenting a cue indicating where in space a target is likely to occur, thereby directing attention to the cued location (Posner, 1980). It is possible to find the anatomy influenced by the cue separately from that influenced by the target by using fMRI to trace changes in the blood that specifically follow the cue. This method is called event-related fMRI, and its use has suggested that the superior parietal lobe is associated with orienting following the presentation of a cue (Corbetta & Shulman, 2002). The superior parietal lobe in humans is closely related to the lateral intraparietal area (LIP) in monkeys, which is involved in the production of eye movements (Andersen, 1989). When a target occurs at an uncued location and attention has to be disengaged and moved to a new location, there is activity in the temporal parietal junction (Corbetta & Shulman, 2002). Lesions of the temporal parietal junction and superior temporal lobe have been consistently related to difficulties in orienting (Karnath, Ferber, & Himmelbach, 2001).

Executive control of attention is often studied by tasks that involve conflict, such as various versions of the Stroop task. These conflict tasks are thought to provide insight into the everyday problem of resolving conflicts among the many brain areas that may be active simultaneously, in order to maintain a coherent direction of behavior. In the Stroop task, subjects must respond to the color of ink (e.g., red) while ignoring the color word name (e.g., blue) (Bush, Luu, & Posner, 2000). Since in skilled readers, the name of a word is automatically activated, it tends to interfere with saying a different ink color. The Stroop task and other conflict-related tasks have been used to study the resolution between competing response tendencies. Resolving conflict in the Stroop task activates midline frontal areas (anterior cingulate) and lateral prefrontal cortex (Botvinick, Braver, Barch, Carter, & Cohen, 2001; Fan, Flombaum, McCandliss, Thomas, & Posner, 2002). There is also evidence for the activation of this network in tasks involving conflict between a central target and surrounding flankers that may be congruent or incongruent with the target (Botvinick et al., 2001; Fan et al., 2003).

The role of the anterior cingulate cortex (ACC) in modulating sensory input has been demonstrated in fMRI studies showing enhanced connectivity between ACC and the sensory modality to which the person is asked to attend (Crottaz-Herbette & Mennon, 2006). This finding supports the general idea that ACC activity regulates other brain areas. Experimental tasks may also provide a means of fractionating the contributions of different areas within the executive attention network (MacDonald, Cohen, Stenger, & Carter, 2000). In accordance with the findings in neuroimaging and lesion studies (Beauregard, Levesque, & Bourgouin, 2001; Ochsner, Kosslyn, Cosgrove, Cassem, et al., 2001), we have argued that the executive attention network is involved in self-regulation of positive and negative affect (Bush, Luu, & Posner, 2000), as well as a wide variety of cognitive tasks underlying intelligence (Duncan, Seitz, Kolodny, Bor, et al., 2000). This idea suggests an important role for attention in orchestrating the activity of sensory, cognitive, and emotional systems.

Simulating Attention Networks

Quantification has had a high value in psychological research. An advantage of the network approach is that it lends itself to the development of precise computer models that allow both summarization of many findings in the field and prediction of new findings. Currently, symbolic models, such as rule-based systems (Newell, 1990), appear to be a good way to capture data from reaction time and other psychological findings. In these models, cognitive functions are represented as chains of production rules and can be identified with the mental operations postulated by cognitive studies. On the other hand, subsymbolic models, such as connectionist models (e.g., O'Reilly & Munakata, 2000), permit a more biologically realistic implementation of mental operations and closer links to imaging studies.

We have developed the attention network test (ANT) to examine individual differences in the efficiency of the brain networks of alerting, orienting, and executive attention discussed above (Fan, McCandliss, Sommer, Raz, & Posner 2002; Rueda, Fan, et al., 2004). The ANT uses differences in reaction time (RT) between conditions to measure the efficiency of each network. Each trial begins with a cue (or a blank interval, in the no-cue condition) that informs the participant either that a target will be occurring soon, where it will occur, or both. The target always occurs either above or below fixation and consists of a central arrow surrounded by flanking arrows that can point either in the same direction (congruent) or the opposite direction (incongruent). Subtracting RTs for congruent from incongruent target trials provides a measure of conflict resolution and assesses the efficiency of the executive attention network. Subtracting RTs obtained in the double-cue condition (which provides information on when but not where the target will occur) from RTs in the no-cue condition gives a measure of alerting due to the presence of a warning signal. This subtraction is a measure of phasic alerting. However, the time for no-cue trials may also provide a measure related to tonic alerting by showing how well the person stays alert when unwarned that a target will occur. Subtracting RTs to targets at the cued location (spatial cue condition) from trials using a central cue gives a measure of orienting, because the spatial cue, but not the central cue, provides valid information about where a target will occur. The ANT is a quick overall measure related to the three networks, but it can be modified to improve the reliability of the measures and observe interactions between the networks (Fan et al., 2009).

The ANT has been simulated in the symbolic framework of ACT-R (Wang, & Fan, 2004). The ANT task is divided into subroutines. Cue processing involves switching of attention to the cued location. Target processing involves detection of the direction of the arrow in the center and also involves an attention switch and response initiation. Each of these operations is implemented by a chain of production rules. The operations are similar to those discussed in many psychological studies and localized in neurological studies. For example, the switching of attention in response to a peripheral cue or target is thought to be implemented by the temporal parietal junction (Corbetta & Shulman, 2002).

A connectionist simulation of the ANT (Wang & Fan, 2007) is based on a local error-driven and associative, biologically realistic algorithm (LEABRA; O'Reilly & Munakata, 2000). The subroutines of ACT-R are now replaced by specific connections between hypothesized neurons or sets of neurons. These neurons are designed to represent the known properties of specific brain areas. Thus, the orienting network can be designed to reflect the known properties of the frontal eye fields, superior parietal lobe, and temporal parietal junction, and the areas can be connected within the simulation. Simulations do a reasonable job of fitting the known ANT data, although improvement can be expected in the future. The symbolic model makes contact with the mental operations related to imaging, whereas the connectionist framework allows for a more detailed view of the underlying biology. Together they illustrate how network views provide a computational means for summarizing many findings within psychology, allowing novel predictions reflecting properties of the network.

INDIVIDUAL EFFICIENCY

Psychology is often divided into two approaches that are almost completely separate in the literature (but see Gardner, 1983, for an early effort at integration). We have been discussing general features of the human mind, such as the ability to attend. Another approach deals with differences among individuals. These differences may involve cognition, as in the measurement of intelligence, or they may involve temperamental differences, many of which relate to energetic factors such as the expression and control of emotions. Almost all studies of attention have been concerned with either the general abilities involved or with the effects of brain injury or pathology on attention. However, it is clear that normal individuals differ in their ability to attend to sensory events, and even more clearly in their ability to concentrate for long periods on internal trains of thought.

We used the ANT to examine the individual differences in the efficiency of the alerting, orienting, and executive networks (Fan et al., 2002). In one sample of 40 normal adults, each of these scores was reliable over repeated presentations in the same session. In addition, we found no correlation among the orienting, alerting, and executive scores. However, it is clear that these networks must be related in everyday life, and indeed small changes in the task produce stronger correlations (Fan et al., 2009). Nonetheless, it is possible to consider each network in relative isolation, as we do in the following chapters.

The ability to measure differences in attention among adults raises the question of the degree to which attention is heritable. To explore this issue, the ANT was used to assess attention in monozygotic and dyzygotic same-sex twins (Fan et al., 2001). Strong heritability was found for the executive network, some heritability was found for the orienting network, and no apparent heritability was found for the alerting network. These data support a search for genes in executive attention and in orienting of attention.

We then used the association of the executive network with the neuromodulator dopamine (see Table 1.2) as a way of searching for candidate genes that might relate to the efficiency of the networks (Fossella et al., 2002). To do this, 200 persons performed the ANT and were genotyped to examine frequent polymorphisms in genes related to dopamine. We found significant association of variations in four genes, the DRD4, MAOA, DAT1, and COMT genes. We then conducted a neuroimaging experiment in which persons with different alleles of two of these genes (DRD4 and MAOA) were compared while they performed the ANT (Fan et al., 2003). Groups with different alleles of these genes showed differences in performance on the ANT and also produced significantly different activations in the anterior cingulate, a major node of the executive attention network.

Recent studies have confirmed and extended these observations. In two different studies employing other tasks, the COMT gene was linked to the mental operations related to resolving conflict (Blaisi et al., 2005; Diamond et al., 2004). Different alleles of cholinergic genes were also related to performance on orienting tasks such as visual search (Parasuraman, Greenwood, Fussella, & Kumar, 2005), thus confirming the link between orienting and cholinergic neuromodulators (see Table 1.2).

Hebb (1949) thought that most of the networks involved in higher functions were shaped primarily through experience. We now know that there is a great deal in common among humans in the anatomy of these high-level networks, and thus that they must have a basis within the human genome. It seems likely that the same genes that are related to individual differences in attention are also important in the development of the attentional networks common among people. Some of these networks are also common to nonhuman animals. By examining these networks in animals, it should be possible to test these assumptions further and to better understand the role of genes in shaping networks.

An important necessity in this effort is the development of methods to manipulate relevant genes in specific anatomical locations that are important nodes of a particular network. Usually, genes are expressed in multiple networks so that changes (e.g., gene knockouts) are not specific to one network. However, subtractive genomics is a method currently being developed to provide greater specificity (Dumas et al., 2005). It is possible that this kind of genetic analysis of network development will become a productive link between genes and both normal and pathological psychological function.

SUMMARY

Attention is an old topic in psychology, but viewing it as an organ system allows the growing exploration of its physical basis. One goal of this volume is to examine the anatomy and development of brain networks of attention. This chapter has defined three networks—alerting, orienting, and executive—and given a summary of the tools used in exploring them. Attention networks are common to everyone, but their efficiency can be measured and it does differ among individuals. These networks are the subjects of the next three chapters. They are each examined by the various tools discussed in this chapter.

Chapter 2

The Alerting Network

BRAIN STATES

The concept of arousal goes back to the classic work of Moruzzi and Magoun (1949) on the role of the brain stem reticular system in maintaining alertness. Lesions of the brain stem reticular system produced an animal in coma. It was thought that the reticular activating system provided the brain state necessary for conscious experience and voluntary action. As more became known about the neuromodulatory chemical systems of the brain stem and thalamus, it was necessary to qualify the general concept of arousal into more differentiated components, such as noradrenergic (norepinepherine), cholinergic, and dopaminergic (see Table 1.2).

I first became involved in alerting during the late 1960s, when I spent a sabbatical year in Cambridge, England. At that time, the distinguished neurologist Grey Walter had shown that a warning signal presented one second before a target produced a sustained negativity, as measured by scalp electrodes that began about 0.5 second after input (Walter et al., 1964). He called this voltage change the contingent negative variation (CNV), because it was obtained when the person was instructed to respond to the target, and he related this finding to the improvement in performance shown when the warning signal indicated there would soon be a target. However, it occurred to me and to Bob Wilkinson, with whom I was working, that many purely behavioral experiments showed RT improvements with very brief warning intervals far less than 0.5 second. If the brain state induced by the warning was responsible, it must be able to begin much faster than 0.5 second. We used much briefer warning intervals and compared the instruction to prepare for a target with one in which the subject simply watched the display and made no response. Using this method, it was clear that the CNV started much more rapidly and was superimposed as a negativity on top of the event-related brain potential elicited by the target. We regarded the event-related potential as related to the warning signal's effect on the sensory pathways and later cortical signals and the CNV as a sign of a change from a less engaged to a more task engaged brain state. Later, Kahneman (1973) described in detail the autonomic changes that were triggered by warning signals. These included the slowing down of heart rate during the period between the warning and the target and the speeding up of heart rate following the target. As will be clear later in this chapter, the CNV originates at least in part from the anterior cingulate, a structure that serves as the gateway to the autonomic system. In 1975, I reviewed the estimated time course of the cingulate and autonomic activities that accompanied the warning (Posner, 1975). The cingulate activity could occur within a hundred or so milliseconds after input, but the heart rate, pupil size, and other autonomic changes occurred later.

Alterations in states of alertness and arousal produced by brain damage are also of interest in clinical neurology. Alertness requires the integrity of brain stem as well as the subcortical and cortical network interactions. Across these many brain regions, several structures appear to have a privileged role in supporting alertness and its variation over the course of the day. Within the brain stem, as judged both by changes in behavior and cerebral cortical activity measured by the electroencephalogram (EEG), specific collections of neurons appear to control arousal states through their balanced interactions. The structures involved include the locus coeruleus, the origin of the brain's norepinepherine system, and other areas of the brain stem and thalamus (Schiff & Finns, 2007).

Closely related to the arousal systems are the mesencephalic reticular formation (MRF) and the thalamic intralaminar nuclei (ILN) that mediate changes in the sleep-wake cycle and modulate sensory processing and higher integrative brain functions. Early experimental observations demonstrate that electrical stimulation of these structures elicited both wakeful EEG patterns and behavioral measures of arousal such as eye opening, vigilant appearance, and autonomic indicators (accelerated heart rate, pupillary dilation).

Acute severe brain injury typically produces one of several brain states. These include coma, an unresponsive state in which a person shows only reflexive motor responses and no sleep-wake variations. Coma reflects overwhelming functional impairment of brain stem arousal mechanisms. Coma may also result from anesthesia or use of other pharmacologic agents. Functional neuroimaging studies suggest that anesthetics exert selective effects on the MRF and thalamus, providing an anatomical overlap with regions that may produce coma based on focal injuries.

The vegetative state (VS) is an unresponsive state in which a person recovers only crude sleep-wake variations with reflexive motor responses and periods when eye opening and closing alternate. Studies of patients meeting the clinical diagnosis of persistent vegetative state, using positron emission tomography, have examined cortical activation patterns in response to simple auditory and somatosensory stimuli. Patients with pervasive VS show brain activations restricted to the primary sensory cortices for both types of stimuli when compared against baseline resting conditions and do not activate higher-order cortical regions engaged by the same stimuli in normal control subjects. These observations are consistent with the understanding that there is widespread functional disconnection across cortical pathways in the VS brain.

The minimally conscious state (MCS) is characterized by limited but observable purposeful responses to the environment but inconsistent evidence for the ability to communicate. Sleep-wake cycles are preserved. MCS patients exhibit fragments of behavior. In contrast to VS patients, however, they demonstrate unequivocal, but typically fluctuating, evidence of awareness of self or the environment, including verbalizations or gestures.

In recent years, neuroimaging studies have revealed islands of preserved function within the brains of some patients in VS and particularly MCS (Owen & Coleman, 2007). They indicate that neuroimaging might be used to reveal partial function in the absence of virtually any observable integrated behavior. Furthermore, these studies have led to efforts to improve patients through the use of deep brain stimulus (Schiff et al., 2007).

The locked-in state (LIS) is characterized by limited but observable purposeful responses to the environment with normal conscious awareness. LIS is not a disorder of consciousness, but it may be confused with VS and MCS. Patients who suffer structural injuries limited to the ventral pontine brain stem may enter into LIS in which only vertical eye movements may remain under volitional control. These patients are fully conscious but behaviorally limited by severe motor disabilities.

The effect of brain lesions in changing the brain state suggests that it is useful to view normal brain states as potentiating forms of conscious experience. One example is the suggestion that the dream state during sleep is potentiated by a brain state in which activity in the brain stem produces the involuntary rapid eye movements (REM) that accompany dreaming. According to Hobson, the dream content may be seen as the results of stimulating semantic memories stored in the brain at a time when the normal stabilizing effects of particular chemical neuromodulators (e.g., norepinepherine) are reduced or not present. This difference in modulators acting on stored memories accounts for the familiar yet bizarre nature of the dream content (Hobson, 1999).

A second example is the hypnotic state, one feature of which is the overwhelming dominance of sensory input over internal self-regulation. In this state, a subject may execute the instruction of another and be unaware of doing so when returned to the normal state. This state may mimic, in part, the early childhood state where the orienting network seems to dominate over the executive network (in Chapter 5, we discuss in detail the evidence for this shift in development).

The existence of these different neurological states demonstrates the importance of the detailed patterns of arousal of the brain in determining the kinds of attention and behavior of which people are capable. Recently, the study of brain states in normal people has become an important topic in fMRI studies within cognitive neuroscience. Raichle et al. (2001) studied the default state when normal subjects are instructed to lie in the scanner in a relaxed state with eyes either open or closed. In this default state, people showed strong activation of brain areas that generally are reduced during task performance. These areas alternated with another network of areas often active during tasks involving attention, including the anterior cingulate and parietal areas. It is not known exactly what these areas are doing when active during the default state, but the state does seem to be common among people, and similar areas are found active in anesthetized monkeys (Vincent et al., 2007). It should be kept in mind that these resting state activations account for much of the metabolic activity of the human brain and specific activations during tasks that involve small (about 5%) changes superimposed upon these background states.

One important approach to understanding the default state is its relation to slow waves found in the EEG. Slow waves such as the CNV are closely related to aspects of fMRI, because both result from synaptic activity that produces local field potentials (Raichle, 2009). After each response in a reaction time task, the person relaxes toward the default state until the next warning signal. Thus, the influence of a warning signal allows for study of the transition between the default state and high levels of alertness during a task.

The ongoing brain state represents a background against which we can examine the influence of specific tasks on the brain and performance. In Chapter 5, we will consider further methods designed to alter the brain state deliberately. During waking hours, the arousal of the brain fluctuates according to a daily cycle (tonic alertness); within this cycle, stimuli can further arouse the brain. In a task such as the ANT, these stimuli include events to which we are to respond (targets) and stimuli that tell us what to expect (cues).

TONIC INFLUENCES ON ALERTNESS

A number of situations have been used to study tonic alertness. These include changes over the course of the day (circadian rhythms). Reaction times are usually longer in the early morning and decline over the course of the day, only to rise again during night and peak in the early morning (Posner, 1975). These measures reflect other diurnal changes such as body temperature and cortisol secretion. A well-established approach to tonic alertness is to use a long and usually rather boring task to measure sustained vigilance. Some of these tasks have come from the job of radar operators looking for near-threshold changes over long periods of time. Vigilance tasks have been shown to rely heavily on mechanisms of the right cerebral cortex (Posner & Petersen, 1990). Both lesion and imaging data confirm that tonic alertness is heavily lateralized to the right (Posner & Petersen, 1990; Shaw et al., 2009). During vigilance tasks, blood flow velocity declines over time in both hemispheres, but this decline is greater for the right hemisphere (Shaw et al., 2009). The no-cue condition of the ANT also seems to measure sustained vigilance because it's a state of relatively low task engagement and would thus be expected to depend more on the right hemisphere.

In alerting, the basis of the attentional influence on arousal appears to be in the locus coeruleus (lc), which is the source of the brain's norepinepherine. Cells in the lc have two modes of processing. One mode is sustained and may be related to the tonic level of alertness over long time intervals. Alertness is influenced by sensory events and by the diurnal rhythm. However, its voluntary maintenance during task performance may be orchestrated in interaction with the anterior cingulate (Posner, 1975; Raichle, 2009; Sturm et al., 2006).

Phasic shifts of alerting can result from presenting any environmental signal. However, if the signal is likely to warn about an impending target, this shift results in a characteristic suppression of the intrinsic brain rhythms (e.g., alpha) within a few tens of milliseconds and a strong negative wave (contingent negative variation) recorded from surface electrodes that moves from midline frontal generators toward sensory areas of the hemisphere opposite the expected target (Rosler, Heil, & Roder, 1997). Alerting, has a surprisingly long time course of development before reaching the adult level (see Table 5.1 p.104).

An extensive imaging study of tonic and phasic aspects of alerting (Sturm & Willmes, 2001) involved a largely common set of both right hemisphere and thalamic areas. Other imaging studies suggest that the warning signal effects rely more strongly on left cerebral hemisphere mechanisms (Coull et al., 2001; Fan et al., 2005). This could represent the common finding on hemispheric differences in which right lateralized processes often involve slower effects (tonic), while left hemisphere mechanisms are more likely to be involved with higher temporal (phasic) or spatial frequencies. The exact reasons for differences in laterality found with tonic and phasic studies are still unknown, but they are important in the interpretation of data, such as in the ANT.

THE PHASIC ALERTNESS STATE

In cognitive psychology, a major emphasis is on producing and maintaining optimal performance during tasks. It is this sense of alertness that is discussed in this section. Hebb (1949) proposed that every stimulus has two effects on the brain. One is mediated by the specific sensory system activated by the signal and the other by its effect on the brain stem arousal system. To examine these effects, it is often useful to use a warning signal prior to a target. If a speeded response is required to the target, reaction time improves for several hundred milliseconds following a warning. The improvement in reaction time is accompanied by marked changes in the state of the organism. These changes are presumably superimposed on the default state, which was discussed above.

Changes in brain state during the time between warning and target reflect a suppression of ongoing activity thought to prepare the system for a rapid response. In the central nervous system, the CNV begins with the warning signal and may remain present until the target presentation. This negative change appears to arise at least in part in the anterior cingulate and adjacent structures (Fischer et al., 2010; Fan, Kolster et al., 2007). The CNV may arise within 100 milliseconds after the warning, in which case it is superimposed on the event-related potential to the warning. If the target interval is predictable, the subject may not show the CNV until just prior to when the target occurs. The alert state is also indexed by widespread autonomic changes such as the slowing of heart rate and an increase in galvanic skin response. This state is a generally inhibitory one and produces a dominance of the parasympathetic autonomic system over the sympathetic system.

How does the alert state influence task performance? Certainly, it does potentiate rapid motor responses to signals. However, it appears to accomplish this in a specific way. The alert state speeds the motor response without altering signal quality. If the input is one that might be missed because it is very short or masked by other input, the probability of detecting the signal is increased by a warning. However, if there is an easily detectable input, speeded reaction time is often accompanied by increased error. This suggests that the response is speeded enough to diminish the quality of information to which the subject responds, thus resulting in increased error rates. I argued that these effects can be understood if the warning signal allows faster input to parts of the brain that mediate conscious detection of the target (Posner, 1978). This idea would allow not only for potentiation of the overt response, but also for the priority of the signal to consciousness.

We are all familiar with high states of alertness that cause rapid responses to targets but also to stimuli that are **not** targets. The linemen in American football sometimes move in advance of the snap of the ball when any flinch by the opponent may produce a reaction. The alert state itself serves to improve processing of all signals. However, when an alerting signal also produces orienting (Chapter 3), the orienting network may inhibit processing of distractors (Corbetta, Patel, & Shulman, 2008).

If information about the nature of the target is known, the sustained electrical negativity related to the CNV will build up over an appropriate brain area. For example, if there is always a visual target to the left of fixation, a standing negative wave will be found over the right parietal region. Because of the hemispheric specificity of the standing wave, it is obvious that this EEG signal can also reflect knowledge of where the target will occur. In this sense, it overlaps with orienting to the target location (Harter & Guido, 1980). The relationship of the CNV to neural activity in the anterior cingulate also suggests its overlap with the executive network. Indeed, activity in the anterior cingulate and related areas (such as the anterior insula) appears to predict performance to detection of a subsequent near-threshold target (Sadaghiani, Hesselmann, & Kleinschmidt, 2009). In addition, slow wave activity is also related to spontaneous changes in the baseline fMRI (Raichle, 2009).

A warning signal triggers neural activity in the locus coeruleus, which is the source of the neuromodulator norepinepherine (NE; Aston-Jones & Cohen, 2005). Warning signal effects can be blocked by drugs such as guanfacine and clonodine, which have the effect of reducing NE release (Marrocco & Davidson, 1998). Drugs that increase NE release can also enhance the warning signal effect. The NE pathway includes major nodes in the frontal lobes and in parietal areas that are in the dorsal part of the visual pathways. However, NE does not influence the primary visual cortex or the more ventral visual pathways. To examine the specificity of the effects to a warning signal, Marrocco and his associates sought to separate information about where a target will occur (orienting) from when it will occur (alerting). To accomplish this, they presented one of four cue conditions prior to a target for a rapid response. By subtracting a double-cue condition (in which the participant is informed of when a target will occur but not where) from the no-cue condition, they get a specific measure of the alerting effect of the signal. When the cue indicating where a target will occur is subtracted from the double-cue condition, the difference represents the effects of orienting. Drug studies with humans and monkeys show that NE release influences the alerting subtraction but not the orienting subtraction, whereas drugs influencing the neuromodulator acetylcholine (ACh) have their effect on the orienting subtraction but not on alerting (Beane & Marrocco, 2004).

There is behavioral evidence that alerting as a general effect on the state of the brain can be separated from specific sensory information concerning the identity of the signal that causes the alerting (Posner, 1978; Kanske & Rueda, unpublished). A visual warning signal (+) was presented prior to presenting a pair of letters, with the subject responding with one key if the letters were the same and another if they were different. The improvement in RT was due to the change in alerting, because the warning provided no information about the match. In a second condition, the warning signal (+) is presented for 0.5 second to bring the person to an optimal alertness, then the first letter is presented, followed after various intervals by a second letter. The improvement in RT following the first letter is due to encoding the identity of the first letter, since alerting is already optimal. Finally, a condition is used in which the first letter is presented without any warning; the letter thus serves as a warning signal and provides information about the identity of one of the match letters. It was found that, for each interval tested, the improvement in alerting and the improvement in pure encoding summed to what happened when the letter served as both warning and part of the letter. Moreover, the same result was found regardless of the complexity of the overall matching task (Posner, 1978; Kanske & Rueda, unpublished).

These results show that, regardless of task difficulty, the improvement in RT from pure encoding as to letter identity and pure warning (alerting) can be added together to get the amount of improvement when a single stimulus produced both functions. This supports the idea that alerting and encoding are separate and largely independent functions. Another finding supports the separation of alerting from the specific sensory information. Following a warning signal, reaction time improves with interval, but errors often increase. The subject attends to the information presented faster, but the quality of information is not better. Therefore, faster responses are associated with poorer quality of information and thus more error. If the first stimulus provides information related to the task on the target, both errors and RT improve at each interval.

As Hebb pointed out, the physiology of alerting rests on the midbrain and thalamic systems, whereas the precise encoding of a stimulus involves cortical sensory systems (e.g., the ventral visual pathway). Neurochemistry provides support for this physiological difference by showing different neuromodulators. There is little or no NE influence directly on the primary visual system or the ventral portion of the visual pathways that is involved in identifying the stimulus (Morrison & Foote, 1986). This anatomy is in agreement with the argument above that the effect of warning signals does not speed encoding of the following target, but rather increases the speed of attention or response to the input signal. However, when a warning also gives information on target location (see Chapter 3), there is evidence that orienting can involve changes within the sensory system of the upcoming target; in this case, both errors and RT improve together. The behavioral findings that individual differences in alerting and orienting are only slightly correlated (Fan et al., 2002; Fossella et al., 2002; see also the next section on development) and that orienting improves to the same degree with a cue regardless of the level of alertness also suggest a great deal of independence between these two functions (Fan et al., 2005). Thus, the physiological and neurochemical separation supports the behavioral separation, even though alerting and orienting function closely together in the tasks of daily life.

DEVELOPMENT

To study individual differences in the brain networks underlying alertness, we developed separate versions of the attention network test (ANT) for adults (Fan et al., 2002) and for children (Rueda et al., 2004), In previous studies, we found that children respond best when there is a story, so in the children's version of the ANT, five colorful fish replace the arrows that typically appear in the flanker task (Rueda et al., 2004). We invite the children to help us feed the fish by pressing a button corresponding to the direction in which a fish is swimming. Visual feedback (the middle fish smiles and some bubbles come out of its mouth) and auditory feedback (a "woohoo!" sound) are provided when the response has been successful. In each trial, the flanker fish are swimming in the same (congruent) or opposite (incongruent) direction as the center fish. As in the adult version, different types of cues are presented before the fish appear, so the efficiency of the three attentional networks can be assayed using the same subtractions previously explained. The ANT does not use language stimuli, so it can be used with children, speakers of any language, patients unable to read, or special populations. In about 20 minutes, the test provides a measure of the efficiency of the alerting, orienting, and conflict networks with reasonable reliability that might be improved with further research. Measuring the three network scores in the same test also allows for assessment of possible patterns of interactions among them. (We do not exclude the possibility that certain psychopathologies or brain injuries would impose a dysfunction on the way the attentional networks interact.)

Using the children's ANT, we have assayed the developmental course of the attentional networks (Rueda et al., 2004). As in the adult data, the children's study also revealed independence between the three network scores. The study allowed for the comparison of the network scores of five groups of children between 6 and 10 years of age. A second experiment compared 10-year-old children with adults on both the adult and children's version of the ANT. Performance measures (RT and accuracy) are fundamental to interpreting the network scores, especially when comparing populations with differences in overall reaction time and accuracy (see Table 5.1 page 104).

Although we use subtraction of RTs in the ANT as a measure of the efficiency of the networks, interpretation of the efficiency of the various networks between groups needs to be made with the full range of reaction time and accuracy data in mind. In general, larger differences between incongruent and congruent RTs mean more difficulty in resolving conflict. This is straightforward if error differences are in the same direction, but interpretation is complex if one group shows larger RT differences while the other group shows larger error differences. In this case, different conflict scores could reflect different strategies of approaching the task, instead of differences in the ability to resolve conflict. A more conservative individual (or group) who opts for being accurate will mainly produce slow responses in the incongruent situation in which the probability of committing an error is higher. This approach results in an increased conflict RT score.

Larger alerting numbers generally arise when one group has difficulty in maintaining alertness without a cue. This is clearly the case in right hemisphere parietal strokes, and children also show more difficulty when no cue warns them of a trial. For example, 10-year-old children have larger alerting numbers than adults, mainly because their times for the no-cue condition are especially long. When no cue occurs, the subject must rely on internal (tonic) alertness; thus, this RT may reflect the more tonic aspects of alertness. This difficulty in children also shows up with time on task. In ANT studies, children often show much longer RTs as the number of blocks of trials increases. This is rarely found in adults. In some cases, larger alerting effects might arise because one group uses a cue more efficiently, perhaps by increased effort. In that case, larger RT differences between no-cue and double-cue conditions may not indicate less efficient performance, but rather better use of the warning. Taking into account RT and error rates for each condition helps to interpret the scores and examine possible differences in strategies between groups.

Developmental studies, such as the one summarized in Table 5.1, involve large differences in overall RT and accuracy. Despite this common decline in RT, each network shows a different developmental course. There is a significant improvement in conflict resolution comparing 7-year-olds to younger children, but a remark-able stability in both RT and accuracy conflict scores from age 7 to adulthood. The orienting score was similar to adult levels at the youngest age studied. The alerting scores show some improvement in late childhood and continued development between 10-year-olds and adults. There is also some evidence that older adults lose the ability to maintain the alert state, and thus their alerting is closer to children's (Fernandez-Duque & Black, 2006).

The long developmental process involved in the alerting score reflects the difficulty children have in maintaining the alert state. This factor both inflates their scores in the no-cue condition and also leads to a sharp upswing in RT as the number of trials required increases. We do not know if these two features of the children's data are correlated on an individual basis, as they should be if they are both due to the same underlying tonic alertness function.

PATHOLOGY

The association of neuromodulators with different attentional net-works (see Table 1.2) has given rise to an effort to relate various receptors and transporters to individual differences in network efficiency. The most active area has used the association between dopamine and the executive network as measured by the time to resolve conflict in tasks such as the Stroop and the ANT (see Chapter 4 for reviews of this work). Chapter 3 considers a some-what similar strategy used to relate several cholinergic genes to aspects of orienting. The association of NE with alerting could lead to a similar strategy, although few studies have directly pursued this. One genetic variation that seems to involve alerting is the alpha-2A receptor gene ADRA2A, which has been associated in some populations with Attention Deficit Hyperactivity Disorder (ADHD; Schmitz et al., 2006; Stevenson et al., 2005; Wang et al., 2006) and also with some learning disabilities (Wang et al., 2006), both of which might reflect alertness problems (see below for discussion of ADHD).

The ANT task is relatively new, but it and its components have been applied to the study of normal aging and several forms of pathology. In one such study (Ferenandez-Duque & Black, 2006), the ANT was studied in young and elderly adults and those suffering from Alzheimer's disease. Both normal elderly subjects and Alzheimer's patients showed increased alerting scores over those found in the young. As in children, these increases seem to reflect difficulty in maintaining the alert state in the absence of warning. The normal elderly subjects and Alzheimer's patients did not differ in alerting scores, although the patients showed much poorer ability to resolve conflict.

Parietal lesions often show neglect of the side of space opposite the lesion. Patients with right and left parietal lesions have been studied extensively by use of a cued detection task similar to the orienting part of the ANT (Posner et al., 1987), although in the ANT task the target appears above and below fixation rather than on the left and right sides. Lesions of the right and left parietal lobes, most often from stroke, produce a deficit in orienting attention to the side of space opposite the lesion. In addition, right, but not left, parietal patients have shown a deficit in maintaining the alert state (Posner et al., 1987).

According to one view, establishing improved alertness is a key to all forms of cognitive rehabilitation following brain injury (Sturm & Willmes, 2001). Clearly, most tasks require at least minimal levels of alertness for successful performance. There have been a number of efforts to study rehabilitation of patients with neglect based on training of alertness. One study (Ladavas, Menghini, & Umilta, 1994) used an arrow cue at fixation central cues to compensate for patients who have had parietal damage, and peripheral cues at the target location to aid those with frontal damage, and found that building on the remaining function provides greater success than attempting to rehabilitate the lost function. Another study (Robertson et al., 1995) attempted to compensate for right parietal damage by use of subsidiary cues that maintain the alert state in these patients. This study provided some support for the loss of alertness specific to right parietal patients. A study with seven neglect patients and three weeks of alertness training showed promising behavioral and imaging results immediately after training, but these results were not maintained after a year-long period (Sturm et al., 2006).

Children suffering from ADHD are often found to show poorer performance with stimuli presented directly to the right hemisphere. This might be consistent with difficulties in tonic alertness. Using a spatial orienting task similar to the orienting portion of the ANT, the most compelling deficit of ADHD children appeared to be a difficulty in maintaining the alert state in the absence of a warning signal (Swanson et al., 1991). Related to this finding, a more recent theoretical approach to ADHD (Halperin & Schulz, 2006) has suggested the importance of early problems in the development of the norepinepherine pathways necessary for tonic and phasic alerting. According to this view, later development of frontal areas allows more voluntary control over alerting and can improve symptoms of ADHD.

Imaging data using the ANT (Konrad et al., 2006) has shown that, compared to controls, children with ADHD show a behavioral deficit in the executive network but no differences in the neural networks underlying any of the attentional networks. In another study (Johnson et al., 2008) using the ANT with a large number of ADHD children and appropriate controls, behavioral deficits were found in both the alerting and executive networks. Thus, it appears that ADHD may involve both an alerting and an executive attention deficit (Johnson et al., 2008). ADHD children frequently suffer from sleep problems, and sleepiness often produces hyperactivity, perhaps in an effort to compensate. Sleepiness also often produces vigilance deficits when long tasks are performed. It may be that ADHD children show some symptoms that arise from a deficit in tonic arousal leading to overcompensation. This would also help to explain the utility of stimulant medication. In future studies of ADHD, more attention needs to be given to commonalities between the alerting and executive networks.

SUMMARY

Brain states related to arousal are an increasingly important topic in cognitive neuroscience. Much of this is due to an examining of the "default state" of brain activity at rest in fMRI. This chapter reviewed the idea of brain states underlying conscious processing arising from studies of patient populations including coma, vegetative state, and locked-in syndrome. The default state in normal people is achieved by an instruction to lie quietly without any deliberate activity and with eyes opened or closed. It shows the importance of intrinsic brain activity in maintaining brain networks. However, as reviewed in this chapter there are many other brain states, and alertness itself creates a special state.

Every stimulus has influence on brain arousal as well as on specific sensory and other systems. The use of a warning signal can separate the brain state related to alerting from activity produced by a target. The ability to measure the key functions of attention is central to using neuroimaging to examine recovery of brain function and to the development of rehabilitation programs. The ANT has been useful in allowing measurement of three brain networks and examining the efficiency of these networks in individuals. Both phasic and tonic aspects of alerting can be examined with the ANT. The tonic alerting function relies heavily on right lateralized mechanisms, while phasic changes involve either bilateral or left-sided brain systems. Although no single measure is right for all situations, this chapter has provided some background in the logic of selecting an appropriate behavioral measurement of alertness as one example of isolating an attentional component.

Chapter 3

Orienting of Attention

The vast majority of studies of attention have involved orienting to sensory events, particularly visual events. A basic distinction in this field is between brain areas influenced by acts of orienting (*sites*) and those that are parts of the orienting network itself, and thus *sources* of the orienting influence. The fact that attentional effects can be obtained in many sensory, motor, and emotional brain areas has led some to believe that attention is merely a general property of all brain tissue. However, whereas all sensory systems can be attended, the brain areas that are the source of these effects are much more restricted to parietal and frontal cortical areas and some subcortical areas. Although this chapter is mostly about vision, the sources of attention effects are similar in other modalities (Macaluso, Frith, & Driver, 2000).

In this chapter, I discuss first the purely behavioral results, then the results of lesion studies, then imaging studies, and finally cellular and molecular genetic studies. One underlying goal in this chapter, as it was in Chapter 2, is to show how each level contributes to the overall picture, sometimes correcting mistakes, sometimes solving problems, and often creating new research opportunities.

BEHAVIORAL STUDIES OF ORIENTING

In 1980, I gave the Bartlett lecture, titling my talk *Orienting of Attention* and describing purely behavioral studies. It was interesting to find years later that, according to Google Scholar, the paper resulting from the lecture (Posner, 1980) has been cited more than 3,000 times, and a book with the same name has appeared summarizing some of the more recent behavioral findings related to it (Ward & Wright, 2008).

In the lecture, I sought to do two things: My first goal was to show that a simple cognitive act of shifting attention from one location to another could be demonstrated by improvement in reaction time (RT) to a target event. In my view, the rest of this chapter also demonstrates that RT studies can provide insights into the functional role of brain systems and thus remain an important tool in the era of cognitive neuroscience. In order to ensure that what we were observing was a shift of attention, we had to control for any motor adjustment that could improve RTs. Eye movements were monitored to make sure fixation was maintained, all the target positions were equally distant from the fovea, and there was only a single key, so performance changes could not be due to differential preparation of the key press.

Despite these controls, we were able to show that within half a second, attention could be summoned by a cue at a particular location, improving performance when a subsequent target occurred there, and if the cue meant that the target was likely at another location, improved performance at that location would follow. This demonstrated both exogenous shifts cued from external stimuli at the location to be attended and also shifts of attention that had to be endogenous because they conformed to an instruction, not to the location of a physical event.

The second goal of the lecture was to open the way to investigate the neural basis of these attention shifts. Mountcastle (1978) and Wurtz et al. (1980) both argued that cells in the parietal lobes of monkeys were related to attention, and I wanted to find a method to determine whether this was true in humans as well and to determine exactly what the cells might do in a functional sense. Both of these goals were realized, as I hope will be clear in the forthcoming sections of this chapter.

It is unnatural to shift visual attention to a location when instructed to keep the eyes fixed. Usually, eye movements and attention shifts go together, but to understand the general mechanism of attention required a purely covert shift, because in many situations where attention is used—for example, when we use attention to search memory—we are not necessarily aided by eye movements or any overt change. If attention is an organ system, it ought to have some independence from sensory and motor systems. Thus, it was very important to know the relationship of eye movements (saccades) to attention shifts.

In one study (Posner, 1980), the person fixated on a position on the edge of a computer screen. The first cue summoned an eye movement to the middle of the screen and a second cue 400 milliseconds later summoned the eyes to the opposite edge from where they began. The crucial trials were target events that occurred while the eyes were centered but expecting a cue to move to the right. At that time, the subject was ready for a shift of the eyes to the right, but was faster to press a key when the target occurred back at the original fixation point, leftward from where he was looking, than when the target occurred where he planned to look next. Thus, during the time when an eye movement was prepared toward the right, attention could be shifted leftward.

Ray Klein investigated what he called the oculomotor readiness hypothesis in two dual-task studies (see Klein, 2008, for a review). He asked whether preparing to move attention potentiated an eye movement, and whether preparing to move the eyes potentiated a manual response. Both answers were negative. Next, he examined whether there was a positive correlation between RTs when cues prepared one for an eye movement and when they prepared one for a covert attention shift. They turned out not to be significantly correlated. Thus, like me, he rejected the oculomotor hypothesis. Later, Rizzolatti and colleagues (1987) revived the hypothesis as the pre-motor theory of attention. Some behavioral studies supported this hypothesis, while others did not. It seemed to me that the simpler situations involving merely target detection usually supported a purely covert shift, while more complex tasks that involved identification of the target did not. The issue is still far from settled, and I felt that purely behavioral data might never be convincing. However, clearer results have now been obtained from cellular recordings that are reviewed later in this chapter.

The findings concerning shifts of attention clearly showed that attention moved prior to saccades and could move even without them. What was at issue was only whether the attention shift depended on eye movement preparation. What did paying attention actually do? The most likely possibility seemed to be that attention was a way of giving priority to information, while foveation added the possibility of getting high-quality acuity from the fovea. However, the covert attention shift did prove to have some effect on the quality of information as well. Work by Carrasco and students (e.g., Montagna et al., 2009) showed that a shift of covert attention, while not substituting for the fovea, could—at least under some conditions—improve the ability to deal with small, detailed high-spatial-frequency information and reduced acuity elsewhere. So, attention could clearly improve both the priority and quality of input.

If one attends to an event and then moves attention elsewhere, the previously attended location is inhibited in relation to other locations that could be attended (Posner & Cohen, 1984). I called this phenomenon inhibition of return (IOR). It too has been the subject of many investigations (Wright & Ward, 2008). Most have replicated the basic phenomenon, and many have tested and often rejected interpretations other than an inhibition of return to an already inspected location. One of the most important extensions of this idea is that inhibition of return serves to improve visual search by reducing the probability of return to already inspected locations. I regard IOR as one of many forms of preference for novelty that are built into our sensory and attentional systems.

It is notable that, although priority assigned to a spatial location by attention is mapped in retinotopic coordinates, IOR moves to new positions as the eye moves (spatial coordinates). This finding suggests that the former is meant to operate within an eye movement, while IOR is meant to operate in conjunction with eye movements. In combination, the priority granted to locations by attention and the IOR to already attended locations provide an exquisite adaptation to the needs of our sensory systems. When we are fixated, we are able to shift attention to examine positions other than at fixation by giving them priority and improving resolution. These covert shifts are faster than eye movements and allow for the scanning of multiple areas even during a single fixation. When attention moves to a new location, the previously attended location is less likely to be rescanned than fresh locations.

Quite a lot can be gleaned from purely behavioral studies, including what use a system might have in the social world. I felt there would be more to learn if studies using RT, such as those described above, actually involved the parietal areas recorded in monkey studies. That link would allow both animal studies and studies of brain lesions to aid in our understanding of human attention.

LESION STUDIES

The study of patients with lesions of the parietal lobes allows for systematic connections between brain systems and attention. As discussed above, these studies involved the use of a cue in an otherwise empty visual field as a way of moving attention to a target (Posner, 1980). Electrodes near the eyes were used to insure that there were no eye movements, and since only one response was required, there was no way to prepare the response differently depending on the cue, making it clear that whatever changes were induced by the cue were covert and not due to motor adjustment of the eyes or hand.

The movement of a covert attention shift had been observed by changes in RT. As described in Chapter 1, Shulman, Remington, and McClean (1979) showed that response times to probes at intermediate locations were enhanced at intermediate times, as though attention actually moved through the space. Whether attention moves through the intermediate space is still a disputed matter (LaBerge, 1995), suggesting another limitation of purely behavioral studies.

In the late 70s and early 80s, a number of papers were published using cellular recording to study the properties of cells in the posterior parietal lobe of the monkey (Mountcastle, 1978; Wurtz, Goldberg, & Robinson, 1980). These papers suggested the possibility of attention cells in the parietal cortex that might be critically involved in orienting attention toward visual events. A Tuesday night meeting of our research group had been assigned to read these papers. I asked if we were measuring, with RT behavior that results from such attention cells. I thought that, if the covert shifts of attention in humans could be connected with the monkey studies, it might contribute to linking cognitive psychology to brain mechanisms. I do not think there was much enthusiasm for this idea at the time. After all, cognition was about software, and what did that have to do with the parts of the brain and cells found in monkeys?

In 1979, I met Oscar Marin, an outstanding physician and behavioral neurologist who was about to move to Portland, Oregon, to set up a service and research effort at Good Samaritan Hospital. He invited me to set up a neuropsychological laboratory in conjunction with the hospital. It was a perfect time for me because I had spent the first six months of 1979 in New York working with Michael Gazzaniga, whose career in psychology is probably familiar to most readers, and my brother Jerry Posner, a world-leading neurologist. I mostly tested patients with lesions of the parietal lobe. Gazzaniga had reported that such patients could make same/different judgments concerning objects that they were unable to report consciously (Volpe, LeDoux, & Gazzaniga, 1979). That seemed like something that could be followed up in more analytic cognitive studies. What did a right parietal lesion do that made access to material on the left side difficult or impossible for consciousness and yet still left the information available for other judgments? This is the question I pursued in the new laboratory in Portland. In the end, I commuted to Portland once a week for seven years. It was such a pleasure to work with Oscar Marin that the long drive was worthwhile.

Work with stroke patients shows that lesions of many brain areas result in difficulty shifting attention to locations or objects that were conveyed directly to the damaged hemisphere. In neurology, these patients would be described as suffering from extinction. Extinction refers to the failure of the patient to notice stimuli presented to the lesioned hemisphere when presented at the same time as a similar stimulus to the unlesioned hemisphere. The experimental studies we conducted suggested that we could define different forms of extinction due to lesions of the parietal lobe, the midbrain, or the thalamus (Posner, 1988). These results suggest that lesions to different areas produce a loss of particular mental operations. A mental operation means a component or subroutine of an overall act. For example, in order to shift attention to a new object, one first has to disengage attention from its current focus and move it to the new location where the target can be engaged. Data in the 1980s suggested that operations to disengage (parietal lobe), move (superior colliculus), and engage (pulvinar) were computed in different brain areas that formed a vertical network that performed the task of orienting (for recent reviews, see Losier & Klein, 2001; Corbetta & Shulman, 2011). The idea of localization of mental operations in separate brain areas was appealing because it suggested a solution to the old problem of how there could be localization when widely separated damage could produce the same general behavioral effect (e.g., extinction). It suggested that, to perform an integrated task, the brain had to orchestrate a distributed network of brain areas; yet, the computations underlying a single mental operation were localized to a brain area.

More recent studies of neglect involving both patient and imaging studies seem to support this general approach to localization, but suggest somewhat different separation of the operations involved. As new methods of neuroimaging have become available, they have been applied to the problem of orienting to sensory (often visual) input. The results have helped to clarify how operations are localized. A paradox of the lesion studies in the early 1980s was that the superior parietal lobe seemed to be the area most related to producing a difficulty in disengaging from a current focus of attention, and yet most clinical data seemed to support the idea that clinical extinction arose from more inferior lesions in the temporal parietal junction and/or superior temporal lobe.

Better methods for imaging lesion location helped to reduce this paradox. Lesions of the temporal parietal junction or superior temporal lobe are most closely related to the symptoms of neglect (Friedrich et al., 1998; Karnath, Ferber, & Himmelbach, 2001). When functioning normally, this area allows disengaging from a current focus of attention and thus enables shifting to the new or unexpected event. A lesion in this area is most critical in producing the core elements of the syndrome of neglect or extinction in both humans and monkeys, although the exact location of the most critical area may differ slightly between the two species. In addition, there is much clinical and imaging evidence of lateralization in humans, in that the right temporal parietal junction is more important for disengaging attention than the left (Corbetta, Patel, & Shulman, 2008; Mesulam, 1981; Perry & Zeki, 2000).

There is evidence from stroke patients and other patient groups that indicates brain areas involved in shifting attention. For example, patients with Alzheimer's disease, involving degeneration in the superior parietal lobe, have difficulty in dealing with central cues that inform them to shift their attention (Parasuraman, Greenwood, Haxby, & Grady 1992). There is also evidence that lesions of the superior colliculus may be involved in the preference for fresh locations rather than locations to which one has already oriented (Sapir et al., 1999). Patients with lesions of the thalamus (most likely the pulvinar) also show subtle deficits in visual orienting tasks, which may be related to the access of the ventral information-processing stream. It seems that a vertical network of brain areas related to voluntary eye movements and to processing fresh input is a critical element of orienting, but a precise model, including a role for all of these areas, is still lacking.

The results of these studies were, for me, a revelation. Patients with different lesion localizations in the parietal and frontal lobes, the pulvinar, and the colliculus all tended to show a clinical syndrome that involves neglect of the side of space opposite the lesion. But in a detailed cognitive analysis, it was clear that they differed in showing deficits in specific mental operations involved in shifting attention (Posner, 1988). As I saw it at the time, we had found a new form of brain localization: Different brain areas executed individual mental operations or computations, such as disengaging from the current focus of attention (parietal lobe), moving or changing the index of attention (colliculus), and engaging the subsequent target (pulvinar). It's no wonder that Lashley (1929) thought the whole brain was involved in mental tasks. It was **not** the whole brain, but a widely dispersed network of quite localized neural areas. Even looking back from the perspective of 20 years, I can again feel the excitement I experienced surrounding this idea at the time.

IMAGING STUDIES

Lassen, Ingvar, and Skinhoj (1978) reported changes in cerebral blood flow in the brain when subjects were reading silently. In cognitive psychology, reading had been well studied. Cognitive psychologists knew something about the orthographic, phonological, and semantic operations that must have been taking place while reading, but they would all be combined in the overall blood flow during the reading of passages. Even more compelling for the possible anatomy of mental operations was a paper by Per Roland (Roland & Friberg, 1985) indicating that different parts of the brain were active during tasks such as finding a route, carrying out mental arithmetic, and making verbal descriptions. However, even in this paper, there was no effort to uncover the specific operations that might be performed by the brain areas involved.

In 1984, the Washington University School of Medicine started a national search for a psychologist who might work in conjunction with the developing positron emission tomography (PET) center led by Marc Raichle. It might be surprising to people how reluctant psychologists were to take a chance on brain imaging at that time. For me, this was the opportunity to test the idea that arose from the neurological studies, that individual mental operations would be localized in separate brain tissue. Raichle and his colleagues at Washington University recognized the importance of being able to use PET to illuminate questions of higher brain function.

The St. Louis studies did quite a lot for the development of neuroimaging and mostly supported the idea that widely scattered brain areas were involved when any task was performed (Posner & Raichle, 1994, 1998). Some people thought that these areas were specific for domains of function such as language, face stimuli, etc. I have maintained the importance of mental operations without denying that domain specificity may also play a role in understanding localization (Posner, 2004). For example, there has been a lot of dispute in the area of face processing over whether there is a specific face area, because experts in other domains activate the same area when thinking about their domain of expertise.

However, if one thinks about localizations of mental operations, it seems clear that faces and other objects, where we come to recognize individuals via fine distinctions, share operations in common. A similar argument has been applied to the visual word form area (McCandliss, Cohen, & Dehaene, 2003).

I had gone to St. Louis in the hope of pursuing work on attention. When I spoke to neurologists about covert shifts of attention (without eye movements) and then proposed to break the invisible shift into component operations, such as disengaging and moving, I saw eyes glaze over and interest wane. Language studies had the advantage, having operations that were more concrete and the fact that neurosurgeons valued knowledge about the localization of language areas to aid them in avoiding such areas during surgery. Our language studies (Petersen, Fox, Posner, Mintun, & Raichle, 1987; Posner, Petersen, Fox, & Raichle, 1988) did indicate some brain areas that appeared to be involved in attention. Together with the lesion studies we had already done, it was sufficient to lead us to develop a neural network view of attention (Posner & Petersen, 1990; see also Petersen & Posner, in press, for an update). The paper summarized the separate neural networks involved in alerting, orienting, and executive functions of attention, and although much has been learned over the last two decades, it still provides an important perspective on which much of this volume is based.

The imaging group at Washington University was able to recruit Maurizio Corbetta and Gordon Shulman, who have carried out attention studies. Their fascinating review paper (Corbetta & Shulman, 2002) suggests that there is localization of quite separate mental operations within two areas of the parietal lobe. These form a portion of a larger network whose functions are to align attention with the target. A more dorsal set of areas, including the frontal eye fields and superior parietal cortex, is involved in voluntary shifts of attention either from instructions or as part of an interval goal. A more ventral area that included the temporal parietal cortex was important in shifts of attention that followed a target at an unexpected location. In their view, what was similar to the disengage operation was carried out in the right temporal parietal junction and was strongly lateralized. These findings fit with the clinical data and have been supported by lesion and cellular data (see below). Although my initial estimates of where each operation was located may not have been correct, the beautiful localized brain areas support the overall localization hypothesis.

SITES AND SOURCES

Normally, all sensory events act both to contribute to a state of alertness and to orient attention. In order to distinguish the brain areas involved in orienting from the sites at which they operate, it is useful to separate the presentation of a cue indicating where a target will occur from the presentation of the target requiring a response (Posner, 1978; Corbetta & Shulman, 2002). This methodology has been used for behavioral studies with normal people (Posner, 1978), patients (Posner et al., 1994), and monkeys (Marrocco & Davidson, 1998), both in studies using scalp electrical recording and event-related neuroimaging (Heinze, et al., 1994). A recent version is the cuing approach embedded in the attention network test (ANT) discussed in chapter 1. Two types of cues are of interest for the orienting subtraction. Some cues provide information on when the target will occur. These warning signals lead to changes in a network of brain areas related to alerting, as described in the previous chapter. Other cues provide information on aspects of the target, such as where it will occur, and lead to changes in the orienting network. The best procedure for the study of the covert attention shifts manipulates the validity of the cue, thus allowing one to examine both the advantages of cuing the correct location and the costs of shifting to a new location from one incorrectly cued. Unfortunately, in order to reduce the total number of trials and relieve the burden on patients and young children, the original version of the ANT did not use a validity manipulation. Some modifications of the ANT have corrected this by using the validity manipulation (Fan et al., 2009).

The development of event-related fMRI made it possible to separate the neural activity following a cue from that following a target. This methodological advance allowed one to ask exactly what was done following a cue and what was done following a target. Studies using event-related fMRI have shown that, following the presentation of the cue and before the target is presented, a network of brain areas becomes active (see Hillyard, Di Russo, Martinez, 2004, for a review). This is what is called the *orienting network*. There is widespread agreement about the identity of the areas of the orienting network—including the frontal eye fields, the superior parietal lobe, and the temporal parietal junction— and there is something known about the function of each area.

We know from many behavioral studies (Van Voorhis & Hillyard, 1977; Wright & Ward, 2008) that, when a target is presented at the cued location, it is processed more efficiently than if no cue had been presented. The brain areas influenced by the orienting network will be those normally used to process the target. For example, in the visual system, orienting can influence sites of processing in the primary visual cortex, or in a variety of extrastriate visual areas where the computations related to the target are performed. Orienting to target motion influences area MT (V5), while orienting to target color will influence area V4 (Corbetta et al., 1991). This principle of activation of brain areas extends to higher-level visual input as well. For example, attention to faces modifies activity in the face-sensitive area of the fusiform gyrus (Wojciulik, Kanwisher, & Driver, 1998). The finding that attention can modify activity in primary visual areas (Posner & Gilbert, 1999) has been particularly important because the microcircuitry of this brain area has been more extensively studied by cellular recording than any other.

Event-related imaging studies showed two separate regions of the parietal lobe, both of which can produce difficulty in shifting attention in contralesional space, although for quite different reasons (Corbetta & Shulman, 2002). The temporal parietal junction, particularly on the right side, was important in interrupting the current focus of attention to allow a shift to a new target. For example, this area is active in a cued spatial attention shift when the person is cued to one location but the target occurs at another location. Its operation was therefore similar to the disengage function discussed above, and these imaging findings fit with the evidence that lesions of this area produce the neglect syndrome.

A different region, the superior parietal lobe, seems to be critical for voluntary shifts of attention following the cue. In event-related fMRI studies, this region was active following an arrow cue informing the person to shift attention covertly (without eye movement) to the target (Corbetta & Shulman, 2002). The region is part of a larger network that includes frontal eye fields and the superior colliculus, which appears to orchestrate both covert shifts of attention and eye movements toward targets. During visual search, when people voluntarily move their attention from location to location while searching for a visual target, this brain area is also active.

Most of the studies discussed in this chapter were conducted in nearly empty visual fields so that top-down control could be observed in as simple a situation as possible. Attention generally makes a much larger difference when there are multiple targets among distracters. When multiple targets are presented, they tend to suppress the normal level of activity they would have produced in prestriate areas if presented in isolation (Kastner et al., 1999). This finding has become the cornerstone of one of the most popular views of attention, in which emphasis is placed on competition between potential targets within each relevant brain area (Desimone & Duncan, 1995). This view places less stress on top-down control, or at least emphasizes that top-down control emerges from bottom-up competition.

Cognitive studies of visual search involve a number of distracters and targets. The neuroscience data suggest that the search objects in an array exert a direct inhibitory effect on each other that can be counteracted by the top-down search. It is nonetheless easy to detect a target among distracters if the target differs from distracters in a single feature, such as color (Treisman & Gelade, 1980). When targets are defined by a combination of features (e.g., a red triangle as target, with red squares and blue triangles as distracters), search time is linearly related to the number of items present in the visual field. It is as though there is a single focus of search, and each item or group of adjacent items has to be searched individually. Moreover, it is not possible to report on multiple attributes from more than one target, although it is easy to integrate multiple attributes of a single target once it is located (Huang & Pashler, 2007).

Orienting generally proceeds serially through the visual field, examining one of a small group of adjacent potential targets at a time. Behavioral studies have been ambiguous as to whether it is possible to divide attention between multiple noncontiguous target locations (Wright & Ward, 2008). It appears from studies of people with lesions of the commissures connecting the parietal lobes that the single focus of attention is maintained by mutual inhibition between the two parietal lobes. People with lesions of these connections search more slowly than those without such lesions, but they do seem to be able to divide their search, with each hemisphere searching targets independently (Luck et al., 1989, 1994). Whether normal subjects can turn off this inhibition voluntarily to allow independent search of multiple objects is still disputed. It is clearly possible to track multiple objects when they move slowly in the visual field (Pylyshyn, 2004); however, this may be done by a tagging mechanism that keeps track without employing attention. Moreover, as things speed up, this ability breaks down, so it is not clear to what degree it represents covert switches of attention between locations.

SENSORY COMPUTATIONS

How are the sources of the orienting network able to influence sensory computations? Anatomically, the source of the orienting effect lies in the network of parietal, frontal, and subcortical areas mentioned above. However, the influence of attention is on the signal arriving in sensory-specific areas—for vision, in the primary visual cortex and extrastriate areas moving forward toward the anterior temporal lobe. It appears that this remote influence involves synchronization between activity in the more dorsal attention areas and the more ventral visual areas (Womelsdorf et al., 2007). The synchronization apparently leads to greater sensitivity in the visual system, allowing increased response to targets there and thus improved priority for processing them.

Many studies of orienting using fMRI have shown that, beyond the orienting network, there is also activity to be found in the anterior cingulate, an area critical to executive control, as will be detailed in the next chapter. An important imaging study by Shulman et al. (2009) showed that an unexpected or novel target will summon the cingulate and related areas, thus involving the executive attention network. This may be one important way that a child develops a connection between the attention networks, thus allowing for improved self-regulation (see Chapter 5).

The methods of neuroimaging have proven critical to testing the general proposition that mental operations involved in a given task were widely distributed among brain areas (Posner & Raichle, 1994). It is likely that we still do not have the final answer as to the exact operations that occur at each location, even in such a relatively simple act as shifting attention to a novel event. Nonetheless, the imaging data provide reconciliation between clinical observations and imaging studies. The results of attentional studies, as with many other areas of cognition, support the general idea of localization of component operations and their temporal orchestration when performing tasks.

CELLULAR STUDIES

There has been continuing interest in the role of the frontal eye fields in this network. Some have argued that covert attention shifts are slaved to the saccadic eye movement system (Rizzolatti et al., 1987), and neuroimaging studies using fMRI have shown that covert and overt shifts of attention involve similar neural areas (Corbetta et al., 1998). However, there appear to be important distinctions at the level of individual cells, with some cells in the frontal eye fields active during saccades and a somewhat distinct population of cells involved in covert shifts of attention (Schafer & Moore, 2007; Thompson, Briscoe, & Sato, 2005). The cells responsible for covert shifts of attention also seem to hold the location of cues during a delay interval (Armstrong, Chang, & Moore, 2009).

These two populations of cells are mixed within the frontal eye fields and, at least to date, have not been distinguished by fMRI. However, the cellular data, like some of the behavioral data summarized previously, indicate that covert attention is distinct from the motor system governing saccades, even though they clearly interact with each other. These findings conflict with the aspect of the motor theory of Rizzolatti (1987) that argues covert shifts are due to programming eye movements, and the findings generally support the independent evolutionary history of the orienting network and attention system. Although attention has close relationships to both sensory and motor systems, it remains distinct.

As suggested by the frontal eye field studies, it is important to be able to link the neurosystem results that suggest brain areas related to attention with cellular and synaptic studies that provide more details as to the local computations. One strategy for doing so is to study the pharmacology of each of the attention networks. A series of pharmacological studies with alert monkeys (which, like humans, are able to use cues to direct attention to targets) have related each of the attentional networks we have discussed to specific chemical neuromodulators (Davidson & Marrocco, 2000; Marrocco & Davidson, 1998). As discussed previously (see Table 1.2), alerting is thought to involve the cortical distribution of the brain's norepinepherine (NE) system arising in the locus coeruleus of the midbrain. Drugs such as clonidine and guanfacine act to block NE, reducing or eliminating the normal effect of warning signals on RT but having no influence on orienting to the target location (Marrocco & Davidson, 1998).

Cholinergic systems arising in the basal forebrain play a critical role in orienting. Lesions of the basal forebrain in monkeys interfere with orienting attention (Voytko et al., 1994). However, it appears that the site of this effect is not in the basal forebrain, but instead involves the superior parietal lobe. Davidson and Marrocco (2000) made injections of scopolamine directly into the lateral intraparietal area of monkeys. This area corresponds to the human superior parietal lobe and contains cells influenced by cues about spatial location; they have been shown to have a large effect on the ability to shift attention to a target. Systemic injections of scopolamine have a smaller effect on covert orienting of attention than do local injections in the parietal area. Cholinergic drugs do not affect the ability of a warning signal to improve performance, so there appears to be a double dissociation with NE involved mainly in the alerting network and ACh (acetylcholine) relating to the orienting network. These observations in monkeys have been confirmed by similar studies in rats (Everitt & Robbins, 1997). It is of special significance in the rat studies that comparisons of the cholinergic and dopaminergic mechanisms have shown that only the former influence the orienting response (Everitt & Robbins, 1997; Stewart, Burke, & Marrocco, 2001).

Relating ACh to the orienting network and NE to the alerting network provides additional evidence of dissociation between the different attentional networks. However, neuromodulators also interact; as in the behavior and imaging studies, it is important to stress that these networks are also integrated into a single overall system. For example, the role of novelty in activating the anterior cingulate shows that orienting can involve both the orienting and executive networks. This connection provides one basis for integration of the networks into an overall attentional system during development. In the next chapter, we examine the frontal executive network and show that it is closely related to dopamine as a neural modulator.

GENETIC VARIATIONS

Increased understanding of human genes, together with the association of neuromodulators with different attention networks, makes it possible to ask about the effects of genetic variation on individual differences in the efficiency of attention networks.

Alzheimer's disease (AD) frequently involves reduction in cholinergic influences on brain networks. Because the orienting network has been related to cholinergic modulation, one would expect to find variation in cholinergic genes to influence this network. One important effort in this direction used the APOE gene, which has been linked to Alzheimer's disease. When patients with early symptoms of this disorder were tested, deficits were found (in comparison to normal controls) in dealing with invalidly cued targets in a cued spatial orienting task (Parasuraman & Greenwood, 2004). The authors extended their findings by testing asymptomatic individuals with different alleles of the APOE gene. They found that those in the APOE4 group, who are at risk for Alzheimer's disease, showed a similar but smaller deficit in cued spatial orienting, as had previously been reported for those suffering from AD. This finding was important in showing that genetic differences can be related to specific attentional components. However, the influence of the APOE gene is very general; it is related to cholesterol transport and can thus have influences on many cognitive systems.

A more specific effort has been to use the finding that orienting is related to the cholinergic system and to examine the role of cholinergic genes on spatial orienting and visual search. In one study (reviewed by Parasuraman & Greenwood, 2004), the pure TT allele of the CHRNA4 gene was found to show less benefit from a cue indicating where in space the target was located—and more costs from an invalid cue—than the CC allele. Similarly, reduced performance was also found for the TT allele in visual search tasks. The CHRNA4 gene had no influence on working memory tasks. Since working memory often involves the frontal executive attention network, this finding supports both the cholinergic influence on orienting and a separation between networks.

SUMMARY

This chapter laid out the anatomical basis for a brain system involved in orienting to sensory stimulation. Orienting involves aligning attention with a source of sensory signals. This may be overt, as in eye movements, or covert, without any movement. Orienting can be manipulated by presenting a cue indicating where in space a person should attend, thereby directing attention to the cued location (Posner, 1980).

As in most neural networks, both posterior and anterior brain areas are involved. There is general agreement on the set of cortical areas that are involved in orienting of attention; it is also agreed that these areas become active prior to sensory areas showing the influence of attention. They thus serve as the source of the attention effects found in sensory systems. Synchronization of activity between the orienting sources and the sensory systems may be the mechanism through which improvements of priority and discrimination of sensory information occur.

The orienting system for visual events has been associated with posterior brain areas, including the superior parietal lobe and temporal parietal junction, as well as the frontal areas (Corbetta & Shulman, 2002). Event-related fMRI following the presentation of a cue (Corbetta & Shulman, 2002) reveals the orienting network as the source of the orienting effect. When a target occurs at an uncued location and attention has to be disengaged and moved to a new location, there is activity in the temporal parietal junction (Corbetta & Shulman, 2002). Lesions of the parietal lobe and superior temporal lobe have been consistently related to difficulties in orienting (Karnath, Ferber, & Himmelbach, 2001).

Although there is much we do not know, it is very striking that the superior parietal areas seem to be involved in voluntary, but not reflexive, shifts of attention. The temporal parietal junction appears to be important for both, but primarily in disengaging when there is a current focus of attention to allow a shift to other brain areas. The importance of this area is shown clinically in the lateralized nature of the neglect syndrome and in the behavioral finding that the disengage operation accounts for the bulk of the increased RT involved in shifting attention.

Taken together, the behavioral and cellular data argue that, although eye movements and shifts of attention interact in behavior, they arise from different underlying mechanisms. There is evidence that covert shifts of attention are modulated by the nicotinic branch of the cholinergic system. The CHRNA4 gene has been shown to account for some of the individual differences in the orienting network. More general genetic influences, such as the APOE gene, have also been reported.

The orienting network provides an important example of examination of a network by behavorial, imaging, cellular, and genetic methods that, to some extent, converge in explaining the physical basis of this form of attention.

Chapter 4

Executive Network and Self-Regulation

The idea of a specific brain network for executive attention began at the very start of using PET to study language. A surprise activation was found in the anterior cingulate but only in the task that required the subject to generate an association. Since this was the most difficult task we used it seemed likely that one of the activations would involve the effort or attention needed to carry out the task. Dr. Jose Pardo asked me what would be the gold standard of an attention task in order to see if it produced similar activity. I responded that it would be the Stroop effect and Pardo carried out such a study (Pardo, Pardo, Janer, & Raichle, 1990). He did find the cingulate activity in a similar area. The Stroop effect involves conflict between color of ink and word name and the word association task could also be seen as inducing conflict between naming the word and the associated use. Subsequently the resolution of conflict became the main theory of cingulate activation (Botvinick et al., 2001). However, activity in the cingulate is also found in many tasks in which it would be difficult to say involved conflict (Bush, Luu & Posner, 2000). We have identified it more broadly with many tasks involving aspects of executive control of which the resolution of conflict is certainly one important one.

Executive control is most needed in situations involving planning/decision-making, error detection, novel responses, and overcoming habitual actions. Because these concepts are somewhat vague, a more explicit version of the idea of executive attention has been developed that stresses the role of the executive attention network in monitoring and resolving conflict between computations occurring in different brain areas (Botvinick et al., 2001). As illustrated in Table 1.1, there are many brain networks that can be simultaneously activated, which can lead to conflicting behavior.

Therefore, a major factor in allowing coherent behavior in the social world is the ability to suppress brain activity that conflicts with current goals. This mechanism allows for what is called *self-control* (in adult studies) and *self-regulation* (in child studies), which is essential to survival. The idea of conflict resolution fits well within the usual meaning of attention's involvement with selection. When one computation is selected, its competitors are less important and are not allowed expression in consciousness or behavior. Although this conflict view may not be adequate to explain all situations involving executive attention, it offers a useful model for summarizing much of what is known and provides justification for the design of tasks that, like the ANT, that attempt to measure the ability to resolve conflict.

This chapter first examines behavioral data that led to the idea of a bottleneck in information processing that produces interference, even from widely different mental operations. More recently, the exercise of executive control has also been associated with fatigue and inhibition of future control operations.

Next, evidence is examined for a functional anatomy revealed by imaging tasks dealing with the resolution of conflict. This functional anatomy seems to fit well with what is known from human and animal studies of the evolutionary specialization undergone by brain areas related to conflict resolution.

Reliable individual differences in this executive attention system are related to the resolution of conflict and can be measured by the ANT. Self or parent reports of the ability of children to control their own behavior can be obtained from questionnaires (Rothbart & Bates, 2006). Both the functional anatomy of executive attention and performance in conflict resolution are correlated with questionnaire measures of effortful control. The self-report scales for effortful control as part of the adult temperament questionnaire are shown in Table 4.1.

Table 4.1 QUESTIONS THAT CONSTITUTE EFFORTFUL CONTROL IN ADULTS (R MEANS WEIGHTING IS REVERSED)

EFFORTFUL CONTROL

Activation Control: *Capacity to perform an action when there is a strong tendency to avoid it*

R.   I am often late for appointments.

R.   I often make plans that I do not follow through with.

      I can keep performing a task even when I would rather not do it. I can make myself work on a difficult task even when I don't feel like trying.

      If I think of something that needs to be done, I usually get right to work on it.

      I usually finish doing things before they are actually due (for example, paying bills, finishing homework, etc.).

R.   When I am afraid of how a situation might turn out, I usually avoid dealing with it.

Table 4.1 CONTINUED

Attentional Control: *Capacity to focus attention as well as to shift attention when desired*

R.   It's often hard for me to alternate between two different tasks.

       When interrupted or distracted, I usually can easily shift my attention back to whatever I was doing before.

R.   When I am happy and excited about an upcoming event, I have a hard time focusing my attention on tasks that require concentration.

R.   It is very hard for me to focus my attention when I am distressed.

R.   When I am trying to focus my attention, I am easily distracted.

Inhibitory Control: *Capacity to suppress inappropriate approach behavior*

       Even when I feel energized, I can usually sit still without much trouble if it's necessary.

       It is easy for me to hold back my laughter in a situation when laughter wouldn't be appropriate.

       I can easily resist talking out of turn, even when I'm excited and want to express an idea.

R.   I usually have trouble resisting my cravings for food drink, etc.

R.   When I'm excited about something, it's usually hard for me to resist jumping right into it before I've considered the possible consequences.

R.   When I see an attractive item in a store, it's usually very hard for me to resist buying it.

       It is easy for me to inhibit fun behavior that would be inappropriate.

The correlation between the ANT conflict score and questionnaires supports the use of self or parent reports in the examination of the role of executive attention in self-control in the social environment. Understanding the physical basis of self-regulation through studies of executive attention gives perspective into the mechanisms of voluntary control and, to some extent, of awareness; both are important components of consciousness.

BEHAVIORAL STUDIES

The idea of a high-level attention system arose in the finding of a general bottleneck in attempting to process information. In my 1978 book, *Chronometric Explorations of Mind*, I summarized findings that at the time supported such a high-level system, which I argued was closely related to our consciousness of the stimulus. Priming studies showed that a stimulus, even if masked from consciousness, could activate associated information stored in memory. However, once the stimulus was selected as a target, there was widespread interference with other stimuli that occur simultaneously or within a short interval.

One example is a task in which a single letter was presented and then followed after a 1-second interval by a second letter. The subject was required to press one key if the letter was identical to the prior one and another key if it was not. A dual task was used in which, when a tone was presented, the person pressed a single key with the hand not used for the letter task. If the tone occurred during processing of the first letter, it was responded to quite rapidly; if it was presented when the second target letter was being processed, there was a drastic interference with the probe tone. These experiments recalled the psychological refractory period studies, which had first suggested a limited processing system (Broadbent, 1958). They differed only in showing that the probe tone could either come before, during, or after the letter task, thus not allowing the person to follow the strategy of always responding to the primary task first.

Interference with probe tasks was greatly clarified by a 1980 experiment by John Duncan. He showed that subjects could monitor several channels simultaneously without interference. That is, the likelihood of finding a target was not diminished by the number of simultaneous locations at which a target might occur. However, if a target occurred on any one channel, a simultaneous target was very likely to be missed. These studies showed that the orienting network could be summoned effectively to whatever channel received stimulation. This reflected the general finding that, when not already committed, the orienting mechanism could be efficiently summoned by any input. The bottleneck only arose when there was some special act of attention to the target that produced interference. Subsequent studies have continued to show that attention can be summoned very efficiently to any target when there is no need to respond to the input, but that, once an item is selected as a target, there is a severe bottleneck.

The bottleneck studies suggest a common brain network involved in processing targets. However, some objected to the bottleneck idea, suggesting that the limited capacity was not due to a limited capacity common mechanism, but rather arose as a result of the need to resolve conflict among possible alternatives so as to maintain coherence in behavior. However, these two views can be complementary, if, as is argued in this chapter, the conflict among response alternatives is the source of interference.

A very different but related approach stresses that the exercise of deliberate self-control can be fatigued by use (Baumeister, Vohs, &

Tice, 2007). In these studies, a subject is asked to exercise control by carrying out a difficult task. It is shown that subsequent exercises of control are inhibited with respect to a control group that is not carrying out the difficult task. In this literature, the exercise of self-control involves a limited resource, and its use results in temporary depletion. Although no studies provide an anatomical basis for this system, it seems likely that it would involve the same anatomy as the executive attention network, because its operation involves self-control. Baumeister and associates (Gailliot et al., 2007) have also argued that utilization of glucose might be the key to the reduction of control with long, continued mental exercise.

FUNCTIONAL ANATOMY

A very large number of functional imaging studies have examined tasks that involve executive attention. These "thinking" tasks often activate a wide range of frontal and sometimes parietal areas. Moreover, manipulations of the content of material have often shown that the same areas may be active irrespective of whether the stimuli are spatial, verbal, or visual objects. This has led some to conclude that the frontal lobes may be an exception to the specific identification of brain areas with mental operations that we have discussed for orienting (Duncan & Owen, 2000). Duncan (2010) has proposed that the regions of the frontal cortex—including the ACC and ventral lateral prefrontal cortex (and perhaps part of the parietal cortex)—operate as a unit on any task involving high-level cognition. The activation of these regions reflects task demands and not any particular content (e.g., color, form, location). Although Duncan does not refer to the activation of this system as being the current focus of attention, but attention is thought to be occupied by variable contents just as Duncan describes. This idea of a general workspace for carrying out psychological tasks has also been a popular one (e.g., Dehaene et al., 2006).

A frontal network, including the anterior cingulate, the anterior insula, and the lateral prefrontal cortex, has been active in different tasks that involve attention when conflict is present and a nonhabitual response is required. One important study (Duncan et al., 2000) examined a wide range of verbal, spatial, and object tasks selected from intelligence tests that had in common a strong loading on the factor of general intelligence (g). These items were contrasted with perceptually similar control items that did not require the kind of attention and thought involved in general intelligence. This subtraction led to differential activity in two major areas, the anterior cingulate and the ventral and lateral prefrontal cortex.

Nonetheless, it is also possible that areas of the prefrontal cortex are specialized for rather general mental operations that are important for a wide variety of tasks. Many imaging studies have been conducted using either the Stroop task or variants of it that involved conflict among elements (Bush, Luu, & Posner, 2000). The Stroop task requires the subject to respond to the color of ink (e.g., red) of a word that specifies a competing color name (e.g., blue). Another frequently used conflict task is the flanker task, which is used as a part of the ANT. In the flanker task, the person is required to respond to a central stimulus (e.g., an arrow pointing left) when it is surrounded by flankers that point either in the same direction (congruent) or in the opposite direction (incongruent). Another type of conflict task involves responding at either a location congruent or incongruent with the stimulus. These three conflict tasks with the same subjects and scanner were used to determine common areas of activation (Fan et al., 2002). It was found that all three tasks activated areas of the anterior cingulate, some of which were unique but had a common focus. In addition, all activated a common area of the ventral prefrontal cortex.

An event-related functional MRI study of the Stroop effect used cues to separate presentation of the task instruction from reaction to the target (MacDonald et al., 2000). Lateral prefrontal areas were responsive to cues indicating whether the task involved naming the word or dealing with the ink color. The cue did not activate the cingulate. When the task involved naming the ink color, the cingulate was more active on incongruent trials than on congruent trials, reflecting the general finding that lateral areas are involved in representing specific information over time (working memory), medial areas, however, are more related to the detection of conflict.

As mentioned at the start of this chapter the first cue to the functional activity in these areas came from studies of generating the use of a word. In a typical version of this task, subjects are shown a series of forty simple nouns (e.g., hammer; Raichle et al., 1994). In the experimental condition, they indicate the use of each noun (e.g., hammer → pound). In the control condition, they simply read the word aloud. The difference in activation between the two tasks illustrates what happens in the brain when subjects are required to develop a very simple thought, in this case, how to use a hammer. Results illustrate that the anatomy of this high-level cognitive activity is similar enough among individuals to produce focal average activations that are both statistically significant and reproducible. One area that is more strongly activated when generating the use of a word is the anterior cingulate gyrus. Presumably this area suppresses the tendency to read the prompt aloud, thus allowing the response associated with the use. When items were more difficult to generate, the activity of cingulate increased. Two additional areas of cortical activation that are more active in the generate condition are in the left lateral prefrontal cortex and the posterior temporal cortex. Both of these areas have been shown to be involved in many tasks dealing with processing the meaning of words or sentences. One idea is that the lateral frontal area holds the prompt work in storage, while the more posterior area looks up the associated meanings. This finding fits with the time course of this circuit (see below). If the left frontal area is required for temporary storage, it is not surprising that it would be active in many different tasks, as found by Duncan.

CIRCUITRY

An examination of the connectivity of the human cingulate cortex (Beckman et al., 2009) shows that there is a great deal of special-ization in portions of the cingulate. This study found nine clusters of connectivity in the cingulate. However, the findings are broadly consistent with previous studies (Bush, Luu, & Posner, 2000) showing that the more dorsal anterior cingulate is connected to frontal and parietal areas and is involved in cognitive functions, including error detection, conflict resolution, and motor processes. The more ventral portions are related to emotion and detection of reward. Pain studies seemed to activate both dorsal and ventral areas of the cingulate.

The time course of these activations can be examined using a large number of scalp electrodes to obtain scalp signatures of the generators found active in imaging studies (Abdullaev & Posner, 1998). When subjects obtain the use of a noun, there is an area of positive electrical activity over frontal electrodes starting about 150 milliseconds after the word appears. This early electrical activity is compatible with being generated by the large area of activation in the anterior cingulate.

A left prefrontal area (anterior to and overlapping the classical Broca's area) begins to show activity about 200 milliseconds after the word occurs. In the initial data, this area was identified with semantic processing because it was active in tasks such as classifying the word into categories, obtaining an association, or treating one type of word (e.g., animal names) as a target, but not in reading words aloud. These empirical findings have proven to be true in much subsequent work (for a review, see Abdullaev & Posner, 1998). However, the findings that frontal areas appear involved in working memory and that the time course of the activation of the lateral frontal area was early (about 200 milliseconds) both make it likely that this lateral frontal area is related to operations such as holding the lexical item in brief storage during the time needed to look up the associated word use. The left posterior brain area, found to be more active during the processing of the meaning of visual words, did not appear as active until a much later time (500 milliseconds). This activity is near the classical Wernicke's area, lesions of which are known to produce a loss of understanding of meaningful speech. We found evidence of the transfer of information from left frontal electrodes to the posterior area at about 450 milliseconds into the task (Nikolaev et al., 2001). Because the response time for this task was about 1,100 milliseconds, there would be time for the generation of related associations needed to solve the task.

Practice on a single list of words reduces the activation in the cingulate and lateral cortical areas (Raichle et al., 1994). Thus, the very same task, when it is highly overlearned, avoids the circuits involved in thought and relies on an entirely different circuitry.

These studies provide further understanding of the functional roles of different brain areas in carrying out executive control. The medial frontal area appears most related to the executive attention network and is active when there is conflict among stimuli and responses. It may be serving as a monitor of conflict, but it is possible that it plays other roles as well (Botvinick et al., 2001). The lateral prefrontal area seems to be important in holding in mind the information relevant to the task. Even when a single item is presented, it may still be necessary to hold it in some temporary area while other brain areas retrieve information relevant to the response. Together, these two areas are needed to solve nearly any problem that depends on retrieval of stored information. Both of these areas could be related to attention, or one might identify only the medial area with attention and the lateral one with working memory. In either case, they begin to give us a handle on how the brain parses high-level tasks into individual operations that are carried out in separate parts of the network.

The cingulate's role in conflict resolution raises the issue of whether it plays a role more generally in self-control/self-regulation. The specialization of different areas of the cingulate for connection to areas related to orienting (dorsal cingulate) and to brain areas related to emotion (ventral cingulate) supports such a role.

Stronger support for the self-regulation idea arises in studies of functional connectivity. One way that the role of the cingulate in self-control can be examined is by using instructions to control arousal during processing of erotic events (Beauregard, Levesque, & Bourgouin, 2001) or to ward off emotional responses to stimuli when looking at negative pictures (Ochsner et al., 2002). The control instructions produce a locus of activation in midfrontal and cingulate areas in comparison with the same materials shown with no control instructions. When people are required to select an input modality, the cingulate shows functional connectivity (the bold responses of the two areas are correlated) to the selected sensory system (Crottaz-Herbette & Mennon, 2006). Similarly, when involved in emotional processing, the cingulate shows a functional connection to limbic areas (Etkin, Egner, Peraza, Kandel, & Hirsch, 2006). These findings support the role of cingulate areas in the control of cognition and emotion. There is also evidence for anatomical connectivity between the ventral cingulate and limbic areas and the dorsal cingulate, parietal, and frontal areas (Posner, Sheese, Oduldas, & Tang, 2007). The conflict theory involves the role of the cingulate in resolving conflict when different responses are simultaneously active. As discussed previously, a related approach emphasizes that the exercise of self-control can be fatigued by use (Baumeister, Vohs, & Tice, 2007), thus reducing its role in subsequent activity. It seems likely that these both involve the anatomy of executive attention.

LESION STUDIES

Classical studies of strokes of the frontal midline, including the anterior cingulate, show a pervasive deficit of voluntary behavior (Damasio, 1994; Anderson, et al., 2000). Patients with akinetic mutism can orient to external stimuli and follow people with their eyes, but they do not initiate voluntary activity. In some cases, lesions of the midfrontal area in children have produced permanent loss of ability for future planning and appropriate social behavior (Damasio, 1994). Early childhood damage in this area can produce permanent deficits in decision-making tasks that require responses based on future planning (Anderson et al., 2000).

However, studies of patients with small lesions confined to the anterior cingulate (Ochsner et al., 2001; Turken & Swick, 1999) often show deficits in conflict-related tasks, but these patients frequently recover from their deficits. This suggests the presence of another anatomical area that might take over the same functions as the cingulate. Cellular data discussed below suggest that the anterior insula may be such an area.

CELLULAR MECHANISMS

The association of the anterior cingulate with high-level attentional control may seem rather odd, because this is clearly a phylogenetically old area of the brain. Although the anterior cingulate is an ancient structure, there is evidence that it has evolved significantly in primates. Humans and great apes appear to have a unique cell type found mainly in layer V of the anterior cingulate and in the anterior insula, a cell type not present in other primates (Nimchinsky et al., 1999). These spindle cells (also called von Economo neurons, after the anatomist who first described them in 1929) also undergo a rather late development, which is in line with the findings that executive control systems develop strongly during childhood (Allman et al., 2005; see also next section). These projection cells are also found in the anterior insula, a brain structure frequently active together with the cingulate. Although the precise function of these cells is not known, high correlations between their number and encephalization suggest a likely role in higher cortical functioning. The proximity of these cells to vocalization areas in primates led Nimchinsky and colleagues to speculate that these cells may link emotional and motor areas, ultimately resulting in vocalizations that convey emotional meaning (Nimchinsky et al., 1999). Although there is as yet no direct evidence linking the cellular architecture of the anterior cingulate to cingulate activity detected during neuroimaging studies, the importance of this area for emotional and cognitive processing (Bush et al., 2000) makes further exploration compelling.

In addition to the common cellular type, the anterior insula and ACC show strong connections during resting fMRI studies and many tasks. These findings suggest that the anterior cingulate and insula are adapted for carrying out high-level control over widely dispersed brain areas.

Knowledge of the existence of special cell types in the executive attention network cannot by itself provide a firm foundation for understanding the role of attention in daily life, anymore than knowing about mirror neurons can really explain empathy and social interaction. However, a plausible cellular mechanism is an important link in understanding how the executive network influences daily life. To further that understanding, it is important to have a convenient way of studying how familial, cultural, and educational structures depend on attention and self-regulation. The study of effortful control fits the bill.

SELF-REGULATION

What do the perception of pain, either physical (Rainville, Duncan, Price, Carrier, & Bushnell, 1997) or social (Eisenberger, Lieberman, & Williams, 2003), processing of reward (Hampton & O'Doherty, 2007), monitoring of conflict (Botvinick, Braver, Barch, Carter, & Cohen, 2001), error detection (Dehaene, Posner, & Tucker, 1994), and theory of mind (Kampe, Frith, & Frith, 2003) have in common? They all activate an area of the midfrontal cortex that includes the anterior cingulate gyrus. Is there a single function that requires all of these important input signals? We have argued that the role of this brain area is to regulate the processing of information from other networks, serving as a part of an executive attention network involved in the control of both cognition and emotion.

Executive attention is a brain network that includes the anterior cingulate cortex (ACC). In adult studies, it is often activated by requiring a subject to withhold a dominant response in order to perform a subdominant response (Posner & Rothbart, 2007a, 2007b). The ability to control our thoughts, feelings, and behavior in developmental psychology is called self-regulation. This is a broad function, not easy to test or model. However, the self-regulatory view fits well with the evidence of brain activation, functional and structural connectivity, and individual differences. Moreover, the self-regulatory view helps us understand how brain networks relate to important real-life functions and provides a perspective into how the shift takes place between infancy, where regulation is under the control of the caregiver, and later life, where self-control is most important. The first step is to examine individual differences in the executive attention network.

Individuality

Our first approach to individual differences in self-regulation used the ANT. As described previously, we used the ANT to examine the efficiency of the three brain networks described in this and earlier chapters (Fan et al., 2002). To measure individual differences in executive attention, we subtracted congruent from incongruent RTs.

In an fMRI study using the ANT, it was found that each of the networks activated the expected regions (Fan et al., 2005). For example, when congruent flanker trials were subtracted from incongruent flanker trials, the resulting images showed a strong activation in the anterior cingulate. The orienting subtraction showed evidence of superior and inferior parietal and frontal activity. The alerting subtraction showed thalamic, frontal, and parietal activity. In addition to these expected activations, some other areas of activation were found, and there was also some overlap in the brain areas activated by different subtractions. Nonetheless, the overall data supported the separate network idea. As discussed in Chapter 1 (see Table 1.2), each of these networks involves different neuromodulators and different genetic variations.

Two other studies have also produced support for separation between the networks. One study used diffusion tensor imaging and the ANT to reveal separate white matter pathways involved in each network. This study showed that individual differences in each network correlated with a different white matter pathway (Niogi & McCandliss, 2009). Another study used scalp EEG recording and abstracted the power in each of several frequency bands that make up the resting EEG (Fan, Byrne, Worden et al., 2007). It was found that each attentional network showed distinct peaks in the power at different frequencies.

Thus, we had a measure of a brain network that we hypothesized served for self-control or self-regulation. Do reports by the self and others of the ability to exercise self-regulation actually reflect the operation of the executive attention network? To understand this, we turn to the study of effortful control in adults in this chapter and in children in Chapter 5.

Effortful Control

The study of temperament had its roots in centuries-old efforts to link individual characteristics to variation in physiological structure. The fourfold typology of the sanguine (positive and outgoing), choleric (bad tempered), melancholic (sad and fearful), and phlegmatic (low emotionality) types of persons based on the bodily humors goes back to ancient Greek and Roman physicians and persisted throughout the Middle Ages and Renaissance. More modern views of individual differences in temperament, stemming from the studies of Pavlov, were related to the brain. Pavlov believed that organisms differed in the strength of their nervous systems and thus differed in the degree to which they would be able to withstand high levels of stimulation. A review of early temperament research can be found in Rothbart (2011). Below we try to relate these temperamental differences to genetic variability among people.

An early British tradition in the study of temperament emphasized self-report measures and the extraction of broad factors from temperament and personality items and scales, rather than ties to the brain. However, beginning in the 1950s, Hans Eysenck attempted to relate the temperament dimensions obtained from self-report scales—in particular, extraversion-introversion and neuroticism—to ideas stemming from the Russian reflex tradition. Eysenck's efforts were carried over and modified by Jeffrey Gray into what he calls the Behavioral Approach and Inhibition Systems. These two systems provide a fundamental basis for thinking about individual differences in behavior.

The application of temperament has been relatively recent within developmental psychology (see review in Rothbart, 2011; Rothbart & Bates, 2006). Clear evidence emerged from early studies that temperament is not a fixed quantity. Although there are correlations between infant temperament and later child and adult reports of temperamental qualities, some aspects of temperament differ greatly between infants and adults. For example, parents report on the ability of their children to regulate their own emotions and behavior at about 3 to 4 years of age and older, but in infancy, regulation is largely due to the caregiver and is not a clear property of children. Rothbart and Derryberry (1981) divided temperament into reactive and self-regulatory dimensions. Although they argued that both aspects of temperament developed over years, the self-regulatory dimensions such as effortful control were especially prone to developmental change.

Dimensions of Temperament

Questionnaires allow for many types of studies with large populations that are impossible for imaging or even cognitive studies to carry out. The researchers who have had the greatest impact on studies of temperament in childhood are Stella Chess and Alexander Thomas and their colleagues in the New York Longitudinal Study (NYLS; Thomas & Chess, 1977; Thomas, Chess, Birch, Hertzig, & Korn, 1963). The NYLS researchers carried out a content analysis of mothers' reports of their children's behavior during the first six months of life, identifying nine dimensions of temperamental variability. More recent research suggests that revision of this list of temperamental dimensions is needed (Rothbart, 2011). Differences in emotional reactivity can be seen in infancy, but children's self-regulatory capacities develop later in the toddler (to preschool periods) and continue to develop throughout the early school years (Rothbart, 2011; Rothbart & Bates, 2006).

Revisions may be required because temperament develops, whereas the NYLS content analysis was based only on individual variability in young infants. The dimensions thus identified characterize children only early in life; later-developing dimensions were not considered. Although temperament researchers had originally believed that temperament systems would be in place very early in development and change little over time (e.g., Buss & Plomin, 1984), it has been found that temperament systems follow a longer developmental course (Rothbart, 1989; Rothbart, 2011).

For example, one of the most important individual differences is in effortful control (Rothbart, 2011), a higher order factor consisting of a number of subscales. In children, it involves subscales of attention focusing, attention shifting, and inhibitory control. For example, caregivers answer questions such as, "When playing alone, how often is your child distracted?" and "How often does your child look immediately when you point?"; adults may be asked, "I can easily resist talking out of turn, even when I'm excited and want to express an idea. The answers are aggregated to form various scales. The effortful control scale exists for older children, adolescents, and adults (shown in Table 4.1), although the subscales differ among the groups.

Rothbart (2011) and her colleagues have examined the role of effortful control in different nationalities, including American, Spanish, and Chinese. They found that, in China, effortful control was negatively related to extraversion (Ahadi, Rothbart, & Ye, 1993), while in the American sample, it was negatively related to sadness and other forms of negative affect. They argued that this was in line with differences in the two cultures at the time the study was done. Americans valued outgoing people and felt that shy, introverted people suffered from depressive symptoms, in China, however, the idea of overenthusiasm and exuberance—standing out from the crowd—was not valued. Effortful control is as important in exercising control of emotions (e.g., positive and negative affect) as it is in cognition. Effortful control is also related to school performance (Checa, Rodríguez-Bailón, & Rueda, 2008) and other cognitive factors. For these reasons, it would be very useful to make a link between effortful control and executive attention. They both seem to reflect the ability of children and adults to regulate their own emotions, thoughts, and behaviors.

Childhood testing offered evidence favoring the correlation between effortful control and measures of executive attention. Executive attention can be measured from voluntary key press tasks involving conflict from about 3 years of age (Gerardi-Caulton, 2000). In one task, Gerardi-Caulton used conflict between an object identity and location to measure individual differences in time to resolve conflict. She found that these differences were correlated with parental reports of effortful control (EC). Similar findings linking parent-reported temperament and EC to performance on laboratory attention tasks have been shown for 24-, 30-, and 36-month-olds (Rothbart, Ellis, Rueda, & Posner, 2003), 3- and 5-year-olds (Chang & Burns, 2005), and in 7-year-olds (González, Fuentes, Carraza, & Estevez, 2001).

More recently, this correlation has been reported in studies of adults. Kanske (2008) required subjects to press a key corresponding to the color of a central target. The target could be of either positive or negative valence, and surrounding flankers could have either the same emotional tone as the target (congruent) or not. The emotional conflict, although formally irrelevant to the task, increased reaction times, produced a larger N200, and activated an area of the ventral ACC, as measured by fMRI. In addition, a self-report measure of effortful control was negatively related to conflict RT, indicating that subjects with more effortful control had a better ability to resolve conflict. Effortful control was also positively related to ventral ACC activity, showing that their better resolution actually required less brain activity associated with conflict. These data provide strong support for the connection between effortful control and emotional conflict and also support the subdivision of the cingulate described above. Finally, this study supports the EEG signature of conflict found in previous studies.

Effortful control has also been linked to the brain areas involved in self-regulation by imaging studies in adolescents (Whittle, 2007). Whittle had 155 adolescents fill out a temperament scale (Ellis, 2002) and also measured the size of different brain structures and their activity. She found that the dorsal anterior cingulate size was positively correlated to effortful control and that the ventral anterior cingulate activity was negatively related to effortful control. The reciprocal relationship between the ventral and dorsal cingulate has also been reported in other imaging studies (Drevets & Raichle, 1998). Executive attention and the ANT executive attention scores have been related to many aspects of child development. Effortful control is related to the empathy that children show toward others, their ability to delay an action, and avoidance of such behaviors as lying or cheating when given the opportunity in laboratory studies (Rothbart & Rueda, 2005). There is also evidence that high levels of effortful control and good ability to resolve conflict are related to fewer antisocial behaviors, such as truancy in adolescents (Ellis, Rothbart, & Posner, 2004).

The ability to measure executive attention through voluntary key press tasks is not present prior to about 2 to 3 years of age, and it is only about this time or slightly later that parents can answer questions about their child's self-regulatory behavior. However, in Chapter 5, we examine a longitudinal study that looked at children 7 months and older, and we discuss changes that take place between infancy and childhood.

Genetic Studies

There is a connection between genetic variation in adults and executive attention/effortful control that reflects the operation of the executive brain network. The association of the executive network with the neuromodulator dopamine (see Table 1.2) was used as a way of searching for candidate genes that might relate to the efficiency of the networks (Fossella et al., 2002). To do this, 200 persons performed the ANT and were genotyped to examine frequent polymorphisms in genes related to dopamine. We found significant association of the *dopamine D4 receptor* (DRD4) gene and the *monoamine oxidase a* (MAOA) gene with executive attention. We then conducted a neuroimaging experiment in which persons with different alleles of these two genes were compared while they performed the ANT (Fan, Fossella, Sommer, & Posner, 2003). Groups with different alleles of these genes showed differences in the ability to resolve conflict, as measured by the ANT, and also produced significantly different activations in the anterior cingulate, a major node of the executive attention network.

More recent studies have built upon these observations. In two different studies employing conflict-related tasks other than the ANT, alleles of the *catechol-o-methyl transferase* (COMT) gene were related to the ability to resolve conflict (Blasi, Mattay, Bertolino, Elvevåg, Callicott, et al., 2005; Diamond, Briand, Fossella, & Gehlbach, 2004). A study using the children's ANT showed a significant relationship between the DAT1 and executive attention, as measured by the ANT (Rueda, Rothbart, McCandliss, Saccamanno, & Posner, 2005). A number of other dopamine and serotonin genes have also proved to be related to executive attention (see Green et al., 2008, Matay & Goldberg, 2004; Posner, Rothbart, & Sheese, 2006; for summaries).

In the previous chapter, we presented evidence that different alleles of CHRNA4 were related to performance differences in the ability to orient attention during tasks involving visual search (Parasuraman, Greenwood, Fossella, & Kumar, 2005), confirming the link between orienting and a cholinergic neuromodulator. In Chapter 2, we argued that alerting was related to a genetic variation related to norepinepherine (Green et al., 2008). The association of each attentional network with different neuromodulators provides a disciplined way of searching for the role of genetic variations in attention. In Chapter 5, we extend this approach to cross-sectional and longitudinal studies of infants and children.

SUMMARY AND IMPLICATIONS

This chapter is an example of progress in understanding the physical basis of a complex psychological function. Self-regulation has been seen as primarily an issue in child development. However, for adults a similar idea termed self-control has been shown to be an important predictor of performance. The presence of a specific neural network underlying these concepts makes it possible to examine the function of various nodes of the network, as was done in this chapter. It also allows study of the developmental and genetic basis of this brain network, which will be reviewed in the next chapter.

The executive attention network also sheds some light on the complex questions of consciousness. The question of consciousness can be divided into our awareness of the world around us and voluntary control of our own thoughts and behavior. Although there has probably been more effort to understand conscious awareness, particularly of the visual world, this chapter has been concerned with aspects of voluntary control. Even though self-regulation does not deal with all aspects of volition and even fewer aspects of consciousness, it is of sufficient complexity and centrality to serve as a model system for illuminating a psychological concept by examining its physical basis. Moreover, the results of our examination of volition also cast some light on aspects of awareness.

Although there is a long tradition of the study of consciousness within Eastern and Western philosophies, cognitive neuroscience provides a somewhat new perspective on *awareness* and *will*, both of which have been central to discussions of consciousness. An important distinction in studies of awareness lies between general knowledge of our environment (ambient awareness) and detailed focal knowledge of a scene (focal awareness; Iwasaki, 1993). Most people believe that they have full conscious awareness of their environment, even when our focal attention is centered on our own internal thoughts. Experimental studies show us how much this opinion is in error. In the study of "change blindness," when cues such as motion—which normally lead to a shift of attention—are suppressed, we have only a small focus of which we have full knowledge, and even major semantic changes in the remainder of the environment are not reported (Rensink, O'Regan, & Clark, 1997).

Change blindness is closely related to the studies of visual search that have been prominent in the field of attention and involve an interaction between information in the ventral visual pathway, which processes object identity, and information in the dorsal visual pathway, which controls orienting to sensory information (Rensink, O'Regan, & Clark, 1997). Visual search tasks have been important for examining what constraints attention provides to the nature of our awareness of a target event. There is clear evidence that attention to a visual event increases the brain activity associated with it, as was reviewed in Chapter 3.

In addition to changes in sensory systems, focal attention to the target of a visual search appears to involve the executive attention network. Imaging studies reviewed in this chapter suggest that, whenever we bring to mind information, whether extracted from sensory input or from memory, we activate the executive attention network. In some studies, a whole set of frontal areas becomes activated together, forming what is called a global workspace. This global workspace becomes active about 300 milliseconds after a target event is presented. It provides the neural basis for a set of information on which a person is currently working in the process of problem solving (Dehaene et al., 2006; Duncan, 2010).

The distinction between awareness and control (will) is traditional in studies of consciousness. However, one form of awareness, focal awareness, appears to involve the same underlying mechanism that is involved in executive control. In this sense, even though some forms of consciousness (e.g., ambient awareness) may have diverse sources within sensory-specific cortices, there is also a degree of unity in the underlying mechanisms involved in focal awareness and conscious control. The distinction between focal and ambient factors in consciousness may help to clarify the sense of awareness present even when detailed accounts of the scene are not possible, as in change blindness.

Chapter 5

Development of Attention Networks

A major advantage of viewing attention as an organ system is being able to trace the ability of children and adults to regulate their thoughts and feelings. We have seen that adjacent areas of the anterior cingulate are involved in cognitive and emotional control. These control systems develop in connectivity over the early life of infants and young children and lead to our ability to regulate other brain networks and thus exercise executive control over behavior. This control critically depends on factors in the social environment, such as parenting. Better understanding of the mechanisms by which control develops and is exercised can provide guidance to parents and society. Critical to this is an understanding of the mechanisms by which control by caregivers during infancy can be shifted to self-regulation by the child.

Over the first few years of life, the regulation of emotion is a major issue of development. Panksepp (1998) lays out anatomical reasons why the regulation of emotion may pose a difficult problem for the child:

One can ask whether the downward cognitive controls or the upward emotional controls are stronger. If one looks at the question anatomically and neurochemically, the evidence seems overwhelming. The upward controls are more abundant and electrophysiologically more insistent: hence one might expect they would prevail if push came to shove. Of course, with the increasing influence of cortical functions as humans develop, along with the pressures for social conformity, the influences of the cognitive forces increase steadily during maturation. We can eventually experience emotions without sharing them with others. We can easily put on false faces, which can make the facial analysis of emotions in real-life situations a remarkably troublesome business.

(Panksepp, 1998, 319)

CROSS-SECTIONAL STUDIES

A critical job for caregivers is to soothe their infant. During the earliest months, the most common method is holding and rocking, but at 3 months and later, parents also use distraction. Experimentally, the ability to orient attention to control distress can be traced to early infancy (Harman, Rothbart, & Posner, 1997). In infants as young as 3 months, orienting to a visual stimulus provided by the experimenter produced a powerful, if temporary, soothing of distress. One of the major accomplishments of early life is developing the means to achieve this regulation on their own.

An early sign of the child's ability to manage cognitive conflict is found in the first year of life. For example, in A-not-B tasks, children are trained to reach for a hidden object at location A, and then tested on their ability to search for the hidden object at a new location B. Children younger than 12 months of age tend to look in the previous location A, even though they see the object disappear behind location B. The previously rewarded location dominates over seeing the object hidden in a new location. After the first year, children develop the ability to inhibit the prepotent response toward the trained location A and successfully reach for the new location B (Diamond, 1991). During this period, infants develop the ability to resolve conflict between line of sight and line of reach when retrieving an object. At 9 months of age, line of sight dominates completely. If the open side of a box is not in line with the side in view, infants will withdraw their hand and reach directly along the line of sight, striking the closed side (Diamond, 1991). In contrast, 12-month-old infants can simultaneously look at a closed side while reaching through the open end to retrieve a toy.

The ability to use context to reduce conflict can be traced developmentally using the learning of sequences of locations. Infants as young as 4 months of age anticipate the location of a stimulus, provided the associations in the sequence are unambiguous. In unambiguous sequences, each location is invariably associated with another location (e.g., 123; Clohessy, Posner, & Rothbart, 2001). Because the location of the current target is fully determined by the preceding item, there is only one type of information that needs to be attended and therefore there is no conflict (e.g., location 3 always follows location 2). Adults can learn unambiguous sequences of spatial locations implicitly, even when attention is distracted by a secondary task (Curran & Keele, 1993).

Ambiguous sequences (e.g., 1-2-1-3) require attention to the current association in addition to the context in which the association occurs (e.g., location 1 may be followed by location 2 **or** by location 3). Ambiguous sequences pose conflict because, for any association, there exist two strong candidates that can only be disambiguated by context. When distracted, adults are unable to learn both ambiguous sequences of 6 lengths (e.g., 1-2-3-2-1-3; Curran & Keele, 1993), a finding that demonstrates the adults' need for higher-level attentional resources to resolve this conflict. In our studies even simple ambiguous associations (e.g., 1-2-1-3) were not learned by infants until about 2 years of age (Clohessy et al., 2000).

Developmental changes in executive attention were found during the third year of life using a spatial conflict task (Gerardi-Caulton, 2000). Because children of this age cannot read, location and identity, rather than word meaning and ink color, served as the dimensions of conflict (spatial conflict task). Children sat in front of two response keys, one located to the left and one to the right. Each key displayed a picture, and on every trial, a picture identical to one of the pair appeared on either the left or right side of the screen. Children were rewarded for responding to the identity of the stimulus, regardless of its spatial compatibility with the matching response key (Gerardi-Caulton, 2000). Reduced accuracy and slowed reaction times for spatially incompatible compared to spatially compatible trials reflect the effort required to resist the prepotent response and resolve conflict between these two competing dimensions. Performance on this task produced a clear interference effect in adults and activated the anterior cingulate (Fan, Flombaum, et al., 2003). Children 24 months of age tended to fix on a single response, while 36-month-old children performed at high-accuracy levels but, like adults, responded more slowly and with reduced accuracy to incompatible trials.

At 30 months, when toddlers were first able to successfully perform the spatial conflict task, we found that performance on this task was significantly correlated with the same toddlers' ability to learn ambiguous associations in the sequence learning task described above (Rothbart, Ellis, Rueda, & Posner, 2002). This finding, together with the failure of 4-month-olds to learn ambiguous sequences, suggested that the use of learned sequences might be helpful in tracing the development of executive attention.

Effortful control is inversely related to negative affect (Rothbart et al., 2001): children and adults reported to have stronger effortful control show less negative affect. While in infancy negative affect is partly controlled by parents presenting novel objects, to which the infant orients, later in life this regulation seems to be internal, perhaps through the generation of positive thoughts. This relationship is in keeping with the notion that attentional skill may help attenuate negative affect, while also serving to constrain impulsive approach tendencies. Empathy is also strongly related to effortful control, with children high in effortful control showing greater empathy. To display empathy toward others requires that we interpret their signals of distress or pleasure. Imaging work in normal subjects shows that sad faces activate the amygdala. As sadness increases, this activation is accompanied by activity in the anterior cingulate as part of the executive attention network (Blair, Morris, Frith, Perrett, & Dolan, 1999). It seems likely that the cingulate activity represents the basis for our attention to the distress of others. Cingulate activity is related to regulation of positive as well as negative affect. The effort to control arousal to a sexually stimulating movie also shows specific activation of this brain network (Beauregard, Levesque, & Bourgouin, 2001).

Developmental studies find two routes to successful socialization. A strongly reactive amygdala indicative of high fear levels would provide the signals of distress that would easily allow the child to have empathic feelings toward others. These children are relatively easy to socialize. In the absence of this form of control, the development of the cingulate would allow appropriate attention to signals provided by amygdala activity. Consistent with the dual-route view of empathy, the internalization of moral principles appears to be facilitated in fearful preschool-aged children, especially when their mothers use gentle discipline (Kochanska, 1995). In addition, internalized control is facilitated in children high in effortful control (Kochanska, 1997). Two separate control systems, one reactive (fear) and one self-regulative (effortful control), appear to regulate the development of conscience.

Individual differences in effortful control are also related to some aspects of metacognitive knowledge, such as theory of mind (i.e., knowing that people's behavior is guided by their beliefs, desires, and other mental states; Carlson & Moses, 2001). Moreover, tasks that require the inhibition of a prepotent response correlate with theory- of-mind tasks, even when other factors, such as age, intelligence, and working memory, are factored out (Carlson & Moses, 2001). Inhibitory control and theory of mind share a similar developmental time course, with advances in both between the ages of 2 and 5.

One function that has been traced to the anterior cingulate is monitoring and correction of errors. One form of conflict was studied by having children play a "Simple Simon" game that asked them to execute a response command given by one puppet while inhibiting commands given by a second puppet (Jones, Rothbart, & Posner, 2003). Children 36 to 38 months of age showed no ability to inhibit their responses and no slowing following an error, but at 39 to 41 months of age, children showed both an ability to inhibit and slowing of reaction time following an error. These results suggest that, between 38 and 39 months of age, performance changes based on detecting an error response. Because error detection has been studied using scalp electrical recording (Gehring et al., 1993; Luu, Collins, & Tucker, 2000) and shown to originate in the anterior cingulate (Bush et al., 2000), we are able to examine the emergence of this cingulate functioning even during infancy; these findings are discussed below in our report of longitudinal research.

We have examined the ANT in children from 6 to 10 years of age, using a version specifically adapted to them. The results (shown in Table 5.1) for children of this age are similar to those found for adults using the same children's version of the task. The children's reaction times are much longer, but they show similar independence between the three networks. Children have larger scores than adults for alerting at least to age 10 and for conflict up to age 7, suggesting that young children have trouble in resolving conflict and even older children have trouble in maintaining the alert state when not warned of the target.

Neuroimaging using MRI can be used on subjects at least by age 7. Children ages 5 to 16 show a significant correlation between the volume of the area of the right anterior cingulate and

Table 5.1 DEVELOPMENT OF ATTENTION NETWORKS*

AGE	Alerting	Orienting	Executive	Overall RT
6	79	58	115	931
7	100	62	63	833
8	73	63	71	806
9	79	42	67	734
10	41	46	69	640
Adults	30	32	61	483

* All studies involve the child version of the attention network test. The numbers for alerting, orienting, and executive networks are from the relevant subtractions described in Chapter 1. The overall reaction times are means of all conditions. (After Rueda et al., 2004).

the ability to perform tasks requiring focal attention (Casey et al., 1997a). In a functional MRI study, the performance of children ages 7 to 12 and adults was studied in a go/no-go task. The go/no-go task requires responding to most stimuli, but inhibiting responding to certain specified stimuli. In comparison with a control condition in which children responded to all stimuli, the condition requiring inhibitory control activated the prefrontal cortex in both children and adults. Also, the number of false alarms in this condition correlated significantly with the extent of cingulate activity (Casey et al., 1997b). This is consistent with the role of the cingulate in error detection.

These studies provide evidence for the development of an executive network during early childhood. Moreover, the development of executive attention contributes to the socialization process by increasing the likelihood of learning important behaviors related to self-regulation and understanding the cognition and emotion of others. It seems likely that understanding the origins of this system in early development could further our understanding of changes in self-regulation.

LONGITUDINAL STUDY

The cross-sectional studies discussed above (see also Table 5.1) provide some evidence for the development of attention during later childhood. We chose to begin a longitudinal study at about 7 months and follow the participants until school age.

The reason we began at 7 months was a finding on the detection of error. Recall that it was at about 3 years of age before children slowed their performance in response to an error, but even infants seem to detect errors by increased looking times.

In this study, infants observed a scenario in which one or two puppets were hidden behind a screen. A hand was seen to reach behind the screen and either add or remove a puppet. When the screen was taken away, there was either the correct number of puppets or an incorrect number. Wynn (1992) found that infants of 7 months looked for a longer period of time when the number was in error than when it was correct. Whether the increased looking time involved the same executive attention circuitry that was active in adults was unknown. Berger et al. (2006) replicated the Wynn study but used a 128-channel EEG to determine the brain activity that occurred during error trials in comparison with that found when the infant viewed a correct solution. Results indicated that the same EEG component over the same electrode sites differed between conditions in infants and adults. Because this EEG component had been shown to come from the anterior cingulate gyrus (Dehaene, Posner, & Tucker, 1994), it appears that the same brain anatomy is involved as in adult studies. Of course, activation of this anatomy for observing an error is not the same as found in adults, who actually slow down after an error and adjust their performance. However, it does suggest that, even very early in life, the anatomy of the executive attention system is at least partly in place.

The development of executive attention can be easily observed by questionnaire and cognitive tasks after about age 3 to 4, when parents can identify the ability of their children to regulate their emotions and control their behavior in accordance with social demands. However, in infancy it has been difficult to word questions that refer to effortful control, because most regulation seems automatic or involves the caregiver's intervention. Obviously, infants cannot be instructed to press a key in accordance with a particular rule. However, the clear evidence on error detection made it seem likely that the attention networks were in place much earlier than we had suspected.

Our longitudinal study involved 70 children from 7 months to 4 years of age. We examined various aspects of temperament and behavior and also asked if the genes we had shown to influence attention in adults would have specific roles in the development of self-regulation during infancy and childhood. We retested and genotyped the children at 2 years of age and tested them again at age 4, when they were able perform the ANT as a measure of executive attention.

Because infants are not able to carry out voluntary attention tasks, we used a visual task in which series of attractive stimuli are put on the screen in a repetitive sequence. Infants orient to them by moving their eyes (and heads) to the location. On some trials, infants showed that they anticipated what was coming by orienting prior to the stimulus. It had been shown previously that infants as young as 4 months of age have a significantly better-than-chance performance in their anticipations (Clohessy, Rothbart, & Posner, 2001), and we thought that these anticipations could be based on an executive attention system and thus serve as an early indicant of executive attention. In agreement with this idea, we found (Sheese et al., 2008) that infants who make the most anticipatory looks also exhibit a pattern of cautious reaching toward novel objects that predicts effortful control in older children (Rothbart et al., 2001, 2003). In addition, infants with more anticipatory looks showed more spontaneous attempts at self-regulation when presented with somewhat frightening objects.

Along with the infants' use of the anterior cingulate in detecting error (Berger, Tzur, & Posner, 2006; Wynn, 1992), these findings suggest that at 7 months they have a rudimentary executive attention system in place, even though parents are unable to report it and infants do not carry out instructed behaviors. However, we found little evidence in tests at 4 years of age that anticipations were related to the executive attention network. Rather, they showed more correlations with orienting than with executive attention (Posner, et al. in press; Rothbart, et al. 2011). This result may reflect the closer integration of the two networks during early development that has been noted in fMRI studies (Dosenbach et al., 2007).

Rothbart and Derryberry (1981) distinguished between reactive and self-regulatory aspects of child temperament. They argued that, early in life, negative affect—particularly fear and orienting of attention—served as regulatory mechanisms that were supplemented by parental regulation. Moreover, Rothbart and Bates (2006) argued for developmental change in which effortful control only arose at about 3 to 4 years of age, when parents could first report on their children's self-regulatory ability.

Our longitudinal study has confirmed but also revised and extended this analysis. We find a negative correlation at 7 months between parent reports of infant orienting of attention and negative affect. Orienting is also positively correlated with reports of positive affect. By 2 years, orienting is no longer related to affect, but effortful control begins to show modest negative correlations with both positive and negative affect.

The results of our longitudinal study along with other findings, discussed below, suggest that, early in life, the orienting network serves as a regulatory system for both negative affect and positive affect, with both orienting and executive networks serving parallel regulatory functions during infancy. Later on, executive attention appears to dominate in regulating emotions and thoughts, but orienting still remains as a control system. This fits well with the view of a parallel control system that is developed in the following sections.

GENES AND EXPERIENCE BUILD NETWORKS

Previous chapters have examined genes related to norepinep-herine that influence the alerting network and those related to cholinergic modulation that influence the orienting network. This section emphasizes the executive network, which is heavily influenced by dopaminergic modulation originating in the ventral tegmental area and interacting with the anterior cingulate and other frontal areas related to executive attention.

We had the children from our longitudinal study return to our lab at 18 to 20 months of age. This time, we added an additional task in which the children played with toys in the presence of one of their caregivers. Raters watched the caregiver/child interaction and rated the parents on five dimensions of parental quality, including degree of support, respect for autonomy, and lack of aggression, according to a schedule developed by NICHD (1993). Although all of the parents were probably concerned and caring, they did differ in their scores, and we divided them at the median into two groups. One of the groups was described as exhibiting higher-quality parenting and the other lower-quality parenting.

DRD4

The dopamine 4 receptor gene (DRD4) has long been related to both attention deficit hyperactivity disorder (ADHD; Swanson et al., 1991, 2000a, 2000b) and, in conjunction with serotonin, the temperamental dimension of sensation-seeking (Auerbach et al., 2001). The DRD4 has several versions that are of relatively high frequency. These differ in the number of repeats of a 48 base-pair part of the gene. Common are 2, 4, and 7 repeats of this portion of the gene. Although the 7-repeat allele of the DRD4 is overrepresented in those with ADHD, it is not related to any deficit in attention as measured by cognitive tasks (Swanson et al., 2000b).

In our children of age 18 to 20 months (Sheese, Voelker, Rothbart, & Posner, 2007), we found no evidence of a direct influence of the 7-repeat on child temperament, but instead found that, in the presence of the 7-repeat, parenting had a large influence on a set of temperamental dimensions that correspond to the symptoms found in children with ADHD. In our longitudinal study, the children did not have any diagnoses of ADHD. The children and their parents seemed representative of our area of the country. Nevertheless, we found that children with the 7-repeat allele who had somewhat lower quality of parenting in our free-play situation had unusually high levels of sensation-seeking (including the dimensions of activity level, high-intensity pleasure-seeking, and impulsivity). In children who did not have the 7-repeat, or those who did but also had the higher-quality parenting, ratings of their behavior on these dimensions were about average.

Because of this finding, we think the paradox of the 7-repeat may arise because its presence can produce symptoms of ADHD without actual attention deficits. However, its presence does not automatically lead to later problems. Whether they do or do not arise depends on features of the environment, such as parenting. Similar evidence that environment can have a stronger influence in the presence of the 7-repeat has been reported by others (Bakermans-Kranenburg & van Ijzendoorn, 2006; van Ijzendoorn & Bakermans-Kranenburg, 2006). All of these findings are reinforced by a study in which children were randomly assigned to parent interventions (Bakersmans-Kranenburg et al., 2008). Those with the 7-repeat showed significant improvements due to the intervention, whereas those without the 7-repeat did not. The use of random assignment of children to groups shows that, in this case, those with the 7-repeat are more influenced by the training. The special susceptibility of those with the 7-repeat may also extend to adulthood. In one study (Larsen et al., 2010), it was found that those carrying the 7-repeat were more influenced in their alcohol consumption by the drinking of their peers than those without the 7-repeat.

An important feature of the 7-repeat is that it appears to have been under positive selection pressure during the past 50,000 years of human evolution (Ding et al., 2002). Theories of positive selection in the DRD4 gene have stressed the role of sensation-seeking in human evolution (Harpending & Cochran, 2002; Wang et al., 2004, 2006). For example, humans leaving Africa might have been especially strong in this characteristic and were therefore successful in coping with aspects of their new environments. Another important idea is that genetic variations such as the 7-repeat may produce unusual vulnerability in one environmental circumstance but also produce improvements in others (Belsky & Pluess, 2009). This idea fits well with the finding that positive selection of the 7-repeat allele could well arise from sensitivity to environmental influences, especially of parents. Parenting allows the culture to train children in the values that it favors, as we have seen earlier in the work in China by Rothbart. In recent years, the nature vs. nurture debate has tilted very much toward the importance of genes, but if genetic variations are selected according to their sensitivity to cultural influences, this could support a more balanced discussion. These new findings suggest that one effect of nature is to influence the susceptibility of the child to his or her environment. A study of the influence of peers on alcohol use suggests that this susceptibility can also influence adult behavior (Larsen et al., 2010). Although this evidence is confined to the DRD4 gene, Belsky and Pluess (2009) have discussed other genes whose effect may be to influence the plasticity of the brain in the face of different environments.

A somewhat surprising aspect of the data on the DRD4 is that its influence on temperament did not appear to be through changes in attention, at age 2. Because our study was longitudinal, it was possible to examine the effects of DRD4 variation in the same children when they were about 4 years old. We found that parenting quality at 18 to 20 months of age influenced effortful control at 4 years of age. The executive attention network is well set up to mediate environmental influence. The anterior cingulate is known to be an important part of reward and punishment networks. Because the dopamine system modulates the activity of the cingulate, the efficiency of the receptor could modify the effectiveness of rewards and punishments. Thus, a system that modulates the reactivity of the cingulate would be well placed to influence attention and behavior.

COMT

COMT (*catechol-o-methyl transferase*) plays an important role in dopamine metabolism by modulating extracellular levels of dopamine. The functional Val/Met polymorphism of COMT has a measurable effect on COMT enzyme activity, with the Val allele degrading extracellular dopamine more quickly than the less enzymatically active Met allele. A finding from our current longitudinal study is that the COMT gene, which has consistently been shown to be related to executive attention in adults and older children, is also related to aspects of executive attention at 18 to 20 months of age (Voelker, Sheese, Rothbart, & Posner, 2009). Haplotypes of the COMT gene influenced both anticipatory looking and other executive tasks at 18 to 20 months of age.

At 7 months of age, COMT was also related to positive affect as reported by parents. The finding of a relationship of COMT to positive affect, together with the influence of this gene on executive attention at 18 to 20 months of age, could provide a genetic link between reactive emotion and emotional regulation during early development. However, it is also possible that COMT's relationship to positive affect in infancy is mediated by regulatory aspects of executive attention. It is likely that the earliest form of executive attention is regulation of emotion, and this may occur in parallel with regulation by orienting. Evidence for this idea is mixed in our current study, in that positive affect in infancy was unrelated to later effortful control, but other studies have shown such a connection (Rothbart, 2011)

CHRNA4

The nicotinic cholinergic receptor CHRNA4 modulates the release of dopamine in the mesolimbic system. As we have seen, in adults this gene has been associated with variation in performance of the orienting network and in brain activity when performing visual attention tasks.

Since visuospatial attention requires orienting, we expected the CHRNA4 polymorphism to influence orienting in our child subjects and thought it might also influence higher-order attention via its relationship with dopamine. At 7 months of age, CHRNA4 is related to more successful anticipatory looking. At about 2 years of age, the main influence of this gene appears to be on effortful control, which depends on executive attention.

In adults, CHRNA4 seems to be related to tasks that clearly involve the orienting network (see Parasuraman & Greenwood, 2004, for a review), but these tasks may involve executive attention as well. In measures of spatial orienting in adults carried out by Parasuraman and Greenwood (2004), the CC allele was related to more benefits from a correct cue and significantly fewer costs from an incorrect one. At 7 months of age, the T/T allele of CHRNA4 is related to better performance in anticipatory looking, but at 18 to 20 months of age, the C/C homozygotes have the highest scores on effortful control (Voelker et al., 2009). At 4 years of age, the C/C homozygotes show more correct anticipations in our visual looking task. It appears that there is an important switch between infancy and age 2 to 4. In infancy, the T/T homozygotes show evidence of better attention, whereas for older children and adults, the C/C homozygotes do better. Below we explore possible explanations for this switch.

Parallel Control Systems

Some studies have examined the brain activity of infants and young children at rest using fMRI (Fair et al., 2009, 2011; Fransson et al., 2007; Gao et al., 2009). These results have shown evidence of sparse connectivity between brain structures during infancy and a strong increase in connectivity at 2 years of age (Gao et al., 2009) and later (Fair et al., 2007, 2009). In studies of neonates, the parietal areas, prominent in the orienting of the attention network, show strong connectivity to lateral and medial frontal areas. By age 2, the anterior cingulate, which has been implicated in self-regulation, shows stronger connections to frontal areas and lateral parietal areas. In work with older children and adolescents (Fair et al., 2009), these tendencies have been shown to continue, and the ACC becomes increasingly differentiated from the orienting network as one approaches adulthood. Fair (Fair, Dosenbach, Petersen, & Schlaggar, in press) says:

> the data suggested that there might be at least two control networks functioning in parallel. Based on the differences in their functional connectivity and activation profiles, we suggested that each network likely exerts distinct types of control on differing temporal scales. The fronto-parietal network* was proposed to be important for rapidly adaptive control and to work on a shorter timescale. The cingulo-opercular network was thought to be important for more stable set-maintenance, and to operate on a longer timescale. Since this initial work, there have now been several reports supporting this framework.

These findings suggest that control structures related to executive attention and effortful control may be present in infancy but do not exercise their full control over other networks until later. Indeed, the connections suggest that initially the ACC has stronger connections to the orienting network and only later becomes differentiated from it. The stronger and early long connections of the parietal areas suggest that, earlier in life, the orienting network may be playing a role similar to the one later associated with the ACC. Error detection activates the midfrontal and/or cingulate areas at 7 months of age (Berger, Tzur, & Posner, 2006) although the ability of infants to take action based on errors seems not to be present until 3 to 4 years of age (Jones, Rothbart, & Posner, 2003).

---

*The fronto-parietal network corresponds roughly in anatomy to what is defined in Chapter 2 as the Orienting network and the cingulo-opercular network overlaps in anatomy with the Executive network discussed in Chapter 4. However, for possible differences in these networks see Petersen & Posner, in press.

These findings fit with the delay in connectivity of the anterior cingulate.

When taken together, the data on resting connectivity and from questionnaires and task performance support both the important role of executive attention as a regulatory mechanism by 18 to 20 months of age, as well as the role of orienting as a control mechanism at 6 to 7 months of age. It seems likely that the parallel activity of these two networks begins in infancy and continues to adulthood. The strong tendency for adults to look away as a self-regulatory strategy suggests a continued role for orienting even for adults. These results fit with the general tendency of infants to be controlled by others in their environment and the remarkable changes that occur in the early years of life that lead to stable self-regulation later. Parents appear to have an important role in this change. fMRI studies of adults show that orienting to novel objects tends to recruit the executive system (Shulman et al., 2009). The use of orienting to novelty by adults as a soothing technique for their infants may play a role in training the executive system. It also seems that the failure of this transition from orienting control to executive control may contribute to forms of childhood pathologies that involve the executive attention network (see Chapter 6). The dominance of the orienting network in infancy and its later switch to executive control may be managed differently in different cultures. Adult work shows that Asian adults pay more attention to context while in the US focal attention is more important (Chua, Boland, & Nisbett, 2005). These differences could relate to how the two systems are trained in early development. It is possible that some brain states (e.g., hypnotism) take advantage of these parallel control systems and the orienting network's close association with sensory input to provide increased control of adult behavior by external events (Posner & Rothbart, 2010). We hope that future longitudinal results and additional studies will provide further information on the coordination between these two regulatory networks.

TRAINING ATTENTION AND SELF-REGULATION

Attention and self-regulation develop under the joint influence of genes and environment. The importance of the transition between control systems early in life raises the issue of whether it would be possible to design experiences that would change the executive network. One possible way of doing this would be to find a way to improve the efficiency of the attention network by strengthening it through exercise (Klingberg, Forssberg, & Westerberg, 2002; Rueda et al., 2005, 2008). This is called attention training, and it is similar to any form of practice. However, in these studies, changes are measured not only by performance but also by the changing efficiency of the brain network involved. Another approach would be to develop a brain state (in the sense discussed in Chapter 2) that would be especially conducive to the ability of the executive network to regulate other networks. In the case of changing a brain state, the changes induced would be present even when the subject is at rest. We call this approach *attention state training* (Tang & Posner, 2009). In our studies, we train attention state through a form of meditation. Some differences between the two methods of training are outlined in Table 5.2. The distinction between attention training and attention state training captures the two major approaches to fMRI through the study either of individual tasks or the correlations among brain networks at rest.

To examine further the role of training on attention networks, a training method that had been used by NASA to train monkeys for space travel was adapted for human children (Rueda et al.,

Table 5.2 COMPARING FEATURES OF ATTENTION TRAINING
WITH ATTENTION STATE TRAINING

Attention Training

- Training of a specific network by repeating an appropriate task

- Requires directed attention and effortful control

- PFC dominant and ACC involvement

- Non-autonomic control systems

- Easy to produce mental fatigue

- Training can transfer to other tasks using the same network

Attention State Training

- Changes body-mind state

- Effortful control (early stage) and effortless exercise (later)

- Autonomic system involvement

- ACC dominant and PFC involvement

- Achieves a relaxed and balance state

- Training transfers to cognition, emotion, and social behaviors

---

2005, 2008). The five-day training intervention used computerized exercises. The effect of training was tested at ages that were within the period of major improvement of executive attention, between ages 4 and 7 years (Rueda et al., 2004; van Veen & Carter, 2002). After training, EEG data showed clear evidence of improvement in network efficiency in resolving conflict. The N2 component of the scalp-recorded averaged electrical potential has been shown to arise in the anterior cingulate and is related to the resolution of conflict (Dehaene, Posner, & Tucker, 1994; van Veen & Carter, 2002). The N2 differences between congruent and incongruent trials of the ANT in trained 6-year-olds resembled differences found in adults. In 4-year-olds, training seemed to influence more anterior electrodes that have been related to emotional control areas of the cingulate (Bush, Luu, & Posner, 2000). These data suggest that training altered the network for the resolution of conflict in the direction of being more like what is found in adults.

The trained group showed an improvement in intelligence compared to the untrained control children. This finding suggested that training effects had generalized to a measure of cognitive processing far removed from the training exercises. No changes in temperament occurred over the course of the training, but this result was expected due to the short time between assessments.

A replication and extension of this study was carried out with 5-year-olds in a Spanish preschool (Rueda, Checa, & Santonja, 2008). Several additional exercises were added, and ten days of training were provided for both experimental and control groups. As in the previous study, the randomly assigned control group viewed child-appropriate videos for the same amount of time that the intervention group was trained. A follow-up session for all children was also given two months after the training. Unlike the control group, the trained children showed improvement in intelligence scores, as measured by the matrices scale of the K-BIT. In addition, the trained group sustained improvement over the two months without further training, while the control group did not. Similar changes in executive attention on EEG were found for the training, as had been observed in the previous study. The training of attention also produced beneficial effects on performance of tasks involving affective regulation, such as the delayed reward test and the Children's Gambling Task (Hongwanishkul, Happaney, Lee, & Zelazo, 2005).

A number of studies with varying methods have been shown to improve attention in preschool children (Diamond, Barnett, & Munroe, 2007; Neville et al., in preparation; Rueda et al., 2005, 2008). Some of these involve classroom training, which may be easier to implement than individual exercises. For example, a year-long training using Tools of the Mind, a curriculum designed to improve executive function, has shown large changes in tasks that measure the ability to resolve conflict. Working memory training, which overlaps heavily with executive attention, has led to improvements in the performance of children with attention deficit disorder (Klingberg, Forssberg, & Westerberg, 2002). This form of training has also been shown in some studies to improve IQ in undergraduate students (Jaeggi et al., 2008).

Many programs that teach specific skills to preschool children do not maintain their advantage when experimental and control children are examined many years later. However, a few skills continue to show an advantage even after several years of schooling. Those skills showing an advantage seem to involve the ability to employ aspects of self-control (Ludwig, 2009). So, although test performance is not maintained for trained children, other aspects of behavior that may be important for success in life after school may continue to favor trained children many years later (Chatty et al., 2010; Ludwig, 2009).

We don't know which exercises are optimal or even better than other methods. Much depends on the goals of the work. Classroom studies are obviously easier to implement in the school situation and they have been shown to alter attention (Diamond, Barnett, Thomas & Munroe, 2007). However, a whole curriculum is complex and does not easily lead to knowledge of what in the training may be the most effective ingredient for change. With the availability of imaging methods, it should be possible to design appropriate programs and activities for children of various ages and with various forms of difficulty. Our studies certainly support the importance of educational design in improving the lives of children. The practical application of brain research to the design of interventions for children has only recently been explored in some detail (Tough, 2008).

ATTENTION STATE TRAINING

The approaches discussed above seek to obtain improvement in networks by exercising them. A rather different approach to training may develop a brain state conducive to self-control. One example is a training method called Integrated Body-Mind Training (IBMT), a form of mindfulness meditation adapted from traditional Chinese medicine (Tang et al., 2007). This method leads to very rapid change with tests involving random assignment of subjects to experimental and control groups. IBMT seeks to develop an optimal state of balance between mind and body. In one study, only five days of group practice were used, during which a coach answered questions and observed facial and body cues to identify subjects in need of help with the method. The trainees concentrate on achieving a balanced state of mind while guided by the coach and a CD that teaches them to relax, adjust their breathing, and use mental imagery.

Because this approach is suitable for novices, it was hypothesized that a short period of training and practice might influence the efficiency of the executive attention network related to self-regulation (Tang et al., 2007). The control group was given a form of relaxation training very popular in the West as a part of cognitive behavioral therapy. In relaxation training, subjects were instructed to relax different muscle groups in turn. They tended to concentrate attention on the instructed muscle group as they relaxed it.

The two groups were given a battery of tests a week before training and immediately after the final training session. The ANT, the Raven's Standard Progressive Matrix, which is a standard culture-fair intelligence test, the Profile of Mood States (POMS), and a stress challenge of a mental arithmetic task, followed by measures of cortisol and secretory immunoglobulin A (sigA), were given before and after training. All of these are standard assays scored objectively by people blind to the experimental condition.

The underlying theory was that IBMT training should improve functioning of the executive attention network by changing the brain state. The experimental group showed significantly greater improvement than the control group in the executive attention network, in mood scales related to self-control, and in cortisol and immunoreactivity measures of stress to a mental arithmetic challenge (Tang et al., 2007). The improvements appear to involve a change of state, in that there is increased brain activity in areas related to the activation and control of the parasympathetic portion of the autonomic nervous systems. Also indicative of a change of brain state is that IBMT alters the resting state (default state), as measured by fMRI.

Further studies revealed the mechanisms underlying this change of state (Tang et al., 2009; Tang et al., 2010). Thirty days of training were used in this study, with neuroimaging used to assay brain changes. The IBMT group had improved its functional connectivity between the ACC and striatum. Moreover, the parasympathetic function had changed more in the IBMT group than in the controls. Further studies using diffusion tensor imaging revealed that several white matter tracts that connected the ACC to other areas had improved their efficiency (Tang et al., 2010).

These tracts include the anterior corona radiate, which had previously been shown to be specifically related to the executive attention network (Niogi & McCandliss, 2009). These findings show that the connectivity related to self-regulation can be altered in adults by training. It has potential implications for all aspects of self-regulation, including clinical and educational applications.

AGING

Results achieved with both attention training and attention state training may indicate that self-regulation may be modified at any age by the appropriate training method. But important issues remain. How long do such improvements last and what are the underlying brain mechanisms changed by these various training methods? Of course, development does not end with young adults. There have been many studies documenting an increase in reaction time with a decrease in accuracy, and a reduction of problem-solving ability and fluid intelligence in elderly subjects when compared to young adults (Salthouse, 2005). Due to the time periods involved, these are generally not longitudinal studies and, like all cross-sectional research, they may be subject to bias in the selection of people at various ages. Despite this problem, studies using modern imaging methods carried out with elderly subjects have provided some insight into changes that occur later in life that are closely related to the brain networks we have been examining.

In one study, Pardo et al. (2007) asked which areas of the brain showed the clearest decline in metabolism with age. They used positron emission tomography to examine metabolism in 46 subjects ranging from 18 to 90 years of age. The strongest association was in the anterior cingulate gyrus. This decline in metabolism in the anterior cingulate may be a reason why aging brings difficulty in self-regulation. However, some studies of aging subjects using the conflict score from the ANT have found no increase in the time to resolve conflict with age, unless the participants had been diagnosed with Alzheimer's dementia (Fernandez-Duque & Black, 2006).

Fair et al. (2009) showed that the connectivity between the anterior cingulate and more posterior brain areas when at rest was very poor in early childhood and showed a marked increase for older children and adults. In a study of resting connectivity in aging adults (Andrews-Hanna et al., 2007), it was also found that connectivity between midfrontal and posterior areas showed a marked decline in old age. Although there was some overlap in strength of connectivity between younger and older adults, the most connected older adult was only at the mean of the younger adults.

While genotype stays constant over the life span, the influence of genes may be even greater in old age than for younger persons. Nagel et al. (2008) examined the influence of the COMT gene on executive attention and working memory. They found genetic effects to be even stronger in the elderly than those found in younger adults. Frontal white matter connectivity has a very long history of development in childhood and adolescence. Thus, the studies of aging tend overall to support the general idea that the connections between brain areas that develop slowly may be especially vulnerable to the influence of aging.

There is evidence that loss in performance and attention with aging can be reduced by various forms of training. Aerobic exercise has shown consistent benefits (Colcombe et al., 2004), but when integrated body-mind training was compared with aerobic exercise in a longitudinal study of ten years' duration, IBMT resulted in improved subjective quality of life and greater activity in the ACC than did physical training (Tang et al., in preparation). These findings suggest the possibility of improving self-regulation among the elderly, but they clearly require larger and more-representative clinical trials.

SUMMARY

In the case of self-regulation, efforts to derive its physical basis depend on the rather surprising relationship between a measure of executive attention derived from the ANT and parental reports of effortful control. The use of conflict in neuroimaging studies has made it possible to discover many nodes of the neural network that carry out resolution of conflict, including the important role of anterior cingulate connectivity in influencing brain areas involved in cognition and emotion. This discovery led to a proposed brain circuitry underlying self-regulation. The anterior cingulate proved to have an important evolutionary history, including the presence of special cells unique to areas involved in self-regulation in humans and great apes. Specialization in this area could well be an important part of the uniquely human ability to delay gratification and to otherwise regulate behavior in the service of long-term goals. This finding provides a renewed opportunity to explore differences between the human and other primate brains.

The association of genetic variations with individual differences in the efficiency of the network provides a further method for discovery of genes that serve to build the nodes and connections of the network during development. This link provides a molecular perspective to the physical basis of a complex psychological construct. The ability to find candidate genes related to the attention network rests on pharmacological findings linking different neuromodulators to the various networks. Other methods, such as the use of full genome scans, the study of brain pathologies, and comparative studies of animals, can also be used to provide appropriate candidate genes.

What illumination will this molecular perspective provide? Evidence for positive selection of alleles of the DRD4 gene within recent human history has led us to propose the possibility that some alleles increase the influence on the child of cultural factors such as parenting. The ability to have greater cultural influence can provide for improved reproductive success and thus produce positive selection. That a molecule can affect cultural influence suggests a strong degree of cooperation between the biological and the social. Although we remain far from a complete understanding of the physical basis of many psychological concepts, the tools currently available appear adequate to foster this effort.

Chapter 6

Attention in the Social World

The social world consists of many institutions in which the ability to regulate our individual behavior in accordance with social demands is of paramount importance. In this chapter, we examine some of the crucial issues of how attention operates in this social world, considering first pathologies that involve attention, and then looking at the role of attention in the education system. Finally, we consider the significance of attention to a number of longstanding issues in cognitive and social neuroscience.

PATHOLOGIES OF ATTENTION

The ability to image the human brain has provided new perspectives for neuropsychologists in their efforts to understand, diagnose, and treat damage to the human brain that might occur as the result of stroke, tumor, traumatic injury, degenerative disease, or errors in development. Because they are now all seen as involving brain networks, the studies of neurological and psychiatric disorders have merged to a surprising degree.

Attentional difficulties are a very frequent symptom of different forms of individual difficulty, ranging from learning disabilities to psychopathology. However, without a real understanding of the neural substrates of attention, there has not been a sufficient basis for systematic efforts to remedy attentional problems. This situation has been changed with the application of our understanding of attentional networks to pathological issues. Viewing attention as an organ system and investigating its underlying neural networks provide new means of classifying disorders that differ from the usual internalizing (e.g., depression) versus externalizing (e.g., conduct disorder) classification applied to such disorders. In next section, we consider the relationship between attention networks and some common disorders. Even though, in general, we do not know whether attention deficits are the causes or the results of a condition, the attention disorder may illuminate the symptoms and suggest methods of prevention and remediation.

Alerting and Orienting

Studies that have used the attention network test (ANT) or other versions of it have been useful in the effort to identify which attention network might be at a deficit in different disorders.

As discussed in Chapter 2, there is evidence that ADHD may involve a deficit in alerting, either alone (Halperin, & Schulz, 2006) or in conjunction with an executive deficit (Johnson et al., 2008). The surprisingly long development of alerting in childhood (see Table 5.1) suggests the possibility that this network could be vulnerable to problems in childhood. Moreover, several studies of children with ADHD have shown deficits that appear to involve alerting (Swanson et al., 1991; Halperin & Schultz, 2006), and the disorder is often thought to show lateralized features of right hemisphere damage that would fit with right hemisphere lateralization of tonic alerting (see Chapter 2). Although ADHD children do not necessarily appear to be sleepy, the hyperactivity they sometimes display may be a compensation for disordered sleep patterns. Hyperactivity is often related to sleep deprivation.

Halperin and Schultz (2006) argue that the cause of the ADHD disorder may be in subcortical modulating systems, but that later in the disorder a patient often gets executive deficits that are the target for drug therapy. In one study using the ANT, ADHD children showed combined alerting and executive attention deficits (Johnson et al., 2008). The executive attention network deficit was also found in adults who had been diagnosed with ADHD as children. When performing a task requiring the resolution of conflict, ADD adults (unlike the controls) did not activate the ACC, but instead showed activation in the anterior insula (Bush et al., 1999). As you will recall, these are two structures that are strongly connected in rest, and both structures are unique in having the special long connections provided by von Economo neurons. If ADHD in adults reduces the efficiency of the ACC, the resolution of conflict might be taken over by the insula (Bush et al., 1999).

In one study of aging using the ANT, normal aging influenced primarily the alerting network, but when aging included Alzheimer's disease, it added an executive deficit (Fernandez-Duque & Black, 2006). As noted in the previous chapter, normal aging was found to reduce ACC function (Pardo et al., 2007), so reduction in executive attention may not be unique to those aged people showing symptoms of dementia. The vulnerability of alerting in normal aging may relate to the late development of the alerting effect in child studies of the ANT described earlier (see Table 5.1).

Autism is most frequently seen as a disorder of social communication. Autistic children fail to reference others, and they have deficits in communication. However, one deficit found in cognitive studies of autistic children is a failure to orient, even when nonsocial cues indicate where in space a likely target will occur (Landry & Bryson, 2004; Townsend & Courchesne, 1994; Townsend, Keehn, & Westerfield, in press). A study using the ANT found that children with autistic spectrum disorders (ASD) showed a significant deficit in orienting but not in other networks. However, the network scores for executive control were also larger in the ASD children, although this was not significant in this study (Keehn, Lincoln, Muller, & Townsend, 2010). An imaging study of cued orienting showed a clear inferior parietal hypoactivity as well as poorer performance (Haist et al., 2005); using a modified ANT, it was found that executive scores can be impaired and imaging showed underactivation of the ACC (Fan et al., in preparation). In the Keehn et al. study, alerting scores were correlated with symptoms of impairment, suggesting the widespread nature of the problems these children face. Deficits in cerebellar and parietal grey matter are also frequently reported in children with autism (Townsend & Courchesne, 1994). An early deficit in orienting could by itself be important in communication problems, as communication critically depends on social referencing. It seems unlikely that autism is confined to a general orienting deficit, because many other brain and behavioral abnormalities have been reported in this complex disorder, but the orienting deficit may provide an important clue to remediation methods.

Several investigators have used tasks that involve valid and invalid cues as a way to study the role of orienting to targets that might be intrinsically negative to the subject (Fox, Russo, Bowles, & Dutton, 2001) or might be associated with punishment (Derryberry & Reed, 1994). The use of a validity manipulation provides better evidence on the specific attentional component involved. Anxiety has often been portrayed as involving heightened vigilance toward objects that might be frightening to a person.

However, these experimental studies using the spatial orienting task suggest that anxious people orient toward negative and positive targets in a similar way, but more anxious people had difficulty in disengaging from the negative target when the cue was invalid. The tendency to dwell on negative targets may be an important aspect of anxiety and depression. Moreover, the specific difficulty in disengaging attention from the negative cue may point to the temporal parietal junction as central to the problem (see Chapter 3). Also possibly related is the finding (Rothbart, 2011) that there is a strong negative correlation between negative affect and effortful control. It is as though stronger attention, probably in this case executive attention, can serve as a protector against depression by making it more likely that the person will be able to disengage from negative ideation.

EXECUTIVE ATTENTION

A number of disorders seem to involve primarily the executive network; these include psychopathy, borderline personality, schizophrenia, and chromosome 22q11.2 deletion syndrome.

Psychopathy

Psychopathy involves a failure of empathy for the pain of others when taking actions that favor the self. Many believe that the initial impetus for empathy lies in the mirror neuron system, which allows the pain of others to be reflected in infant neuronal discharges. However, studies suggest that psychopathic behavior also rests on the degree of attention paid to environmental cues. According to Newman's work, psychopaths who are in prison for their behavior differ from nonpsychopathic prisoners in the degree to which the emotional cues of others will influence their behavior, but only if the situation brings those cues to attention. When cues are not deliberately attended, psychopaths seem to behave similarly to nonpsychopaths, but they do not seem to monitor the environment for those cues if they are not already in the focus of attention (Zeier, Maxwell, & Newman, 2009). It is as though the pain of others is not a salient cue for psychopaths, as it is for normal individuals. According to one imaging study, the ventral ACC was less active in psychopaths when viewing frightening faces than it was for nonpsychopathic individuals (Blair et al., 1999), suggesting that emotional controls are less active in this population, as they themselves report (Baskin-Sommers, Zeier, & Newman, 2009). Another imaging study suggested that the lack of connectivity between executive attention areas and output may be an important factor in psychopathy, thus making a further link between deficits in self-regulation and impulsivity (Shannon et al., 2011).

Psychopathy may have something in common with borderline personality disorder (see next section) in terms of the difficulty in handling emotion. However, the origin of borderline personality disorder appears to be quite early in life, whereas this is less clear of psychopathy.

Borderline Personality

Borderline personality disorder is characterized by great lability of affect and difficulties in interpersonal relations. In some cases, patients are suicidal or carry out self-mutilation. Because this diagnosis has been studied largely by psychoanalysts and has a very complex definition, it might at first be thought of as a poor candidate for a specific pathophysiology involving attentional networks.

However, by focusing on the temperamentally based core symptoms of negative emotionality and difficulty in self-regulation (Posner et al., 2002), it was found that patients were very high in temperamental negative affect and relatively low in effortful control (Rothbart, Ahadi, Hershey, & Fisher, 2001). In our study, a temperamentally matched control group of normal persons was selected who (1) did not meet the requirements for a personality disorder, and (2) were equivalent in scores on these two temperamental dimensions. Comparing their ANT results, a deficit specific to the executive attention network was found in borderline patients in comparison with matched controls.

Imaging results suggested overgeneralization of response to negative words in the amygdala in the borderline patients, and reduced responding in the anterior cingulate and related midline frontal areas involved in self-regulation (Silbersweig et al., 2007). Patients with higher effortful control and lower conflict scores on the ANT were also the most likely to show the effects of therapy. This methodology shows the utility of focusing on the core deficits of patients, defining appropriate control groups based on matched temperament, and using specific attentional tests to help determine how best to conduct imaging studies.

Schizophrenia

A number of years ago, never-medicated schizophrenic patients were tested with a cued detection task similar to the orienting part of the ANT and were studied using positron emission tomography (PET). These patients showed a deficit in orienting similar to what had been found in left parietal patients (Early, Posner, Reiman, & Raichle, 1989). At rest, these subjects also showed a focal decrease in cerebral blood flow in the left globus pallidus (Early et al., 1989), a part of the basal ganglia with close ties to the anterior cingulate. When their visual attention was engaged, they had difficulty in shifting attention to the right visual field, and they also showed deficits in conflict tasks, particularly when they had to rely on a language cue. It was concluded that the overall pattern of their behavior was consistent with difficulties in the executive attention system, with signs mostly of a left hemisphere deficit.

The deficit in orienting rightward has been replicated in first-break schizophrenics, but it does not seem to be true later in the disorder (Maruff, et al, 1995), nor does the pattern appear to be part of the genetic predisposition for schizophrenia (Pardo et al., 2000). As the disorder progresses, the cognitive deficits become more severe and more general. First-break schizophrenic subjects have often been shown to have left hemisphere deficits, and there have been many reports of anterior cingulate and basal ganglia deficits in patients with schizophrenia (Benes, 1999). Benes reported that schizophrenic patients at autopsy showed deficits in outflow from the anterior cingulate, which, she argued, was part of a much larger network of frontal and temporal structures that operate abnormally in schizophrenia (Benes, 1999).

A study using the ANT casts some light on these results (Wang et al, 2005). In this study, the schizophrenic patients were chronic, and they were compared to a similarly aged control group. The schizophrenic patients had much more difficulty resolving conflict than did the normal controls. The deficit in patients was also much larger than that found for borderline personality patients. However, there was still a great deal of overlap between the patients and normal subjects, indicating that the deficit is not suitable for making a differential diagnosis. The data also showed a much smaller orienting deficit of the type that had been reported previously in first-break patients. These findings suggest that, on average, there is a strong executive deficit in chronic schizophrenia, as would be anticipated from the results in Benes's study (1999). It remains to be determined whether this deficit exists prior to the initial symptoms or develops with the disorder.

Chromosome 22q11.2 Deletion Syndrome

This syndrome is a complex one that involves a number of abnormalities in facial and heart structures, but also mental retardation due to deletion of a number of genes. Children with this syndrome are at a high risk for developing schizophrenia. Among the genes deleted in this syndrome is the COMT gene, which has been associated with performance in a conflict task (Diamond, Briand, Fosella, & Gehlbach, 2004) and with schizophrenia (Blasi et al., 2005). In light of these findings, it was expected that the disorder would produce a large executive deficit, and further studies have corroborated this expectation (Sobin, et al, 2004; Takarae, Schmidt, & Simon, 2009). Sobin and colleagues also found that the deficit in resolving conflict is associated with the ability to inhibit a blink following a cue that a loud noise would be presented shortly (prepulse inhibition). The authors suggest that the association of high-level attention and a deficit in prepulse inhibition points to a pathway that includes both the basal ganglia and the anterior cingulate.

PREVENTION AND REHABILITATION

The presence of large individual differences in attention starting in early life and the importance of parenting for behaviors such as activity level and impulsivity suggest that the ability of children to handle a school setting may depend on the joint interaction of genes and environment. As we have seen in Chapter 5, methods of changing attention through direct training or a change of state exist, and these need to be explored as means of preventing disorders that involve attention.

Several training-oriented programs have been successful in improving attention in patients suffering from different pathologies. For example, the use of attention process training (APT) has led to specific improvements in executive attention in patients with specific brain injuries (Sohlberg, McLaughlin, Pavese, Heidrich, et al., 2000), as well as in children with ADHD (Kerns, Esso, & Thompson, 1999). APT involves auditory tapes that direct the patient in tasks involving sustained attention. Work with children with ADHD has also shown that working memory training can improve attention in this population (Klingberg, Forssberg, & Westerberg, 2002; Olesen, Westerberg, & Klingberg, 2004). In nonclinical samples of adults, training with video games has produced better performance on a range of visual attention tasks (Green & Bavalier, 2003).

In addition to efforts to better understand the nature of brain disorders, there have been efforts to adopt ideas related to the physical basis of attention for rehabilitation. Some studies have tried to rehabilitate specific attentional networks (Robertson, 1999; Sohlberg et al., 1997). They are somewhat similar to the child studies cited in Chapter 5. These studies suggest that rehabilitation procedures should focus on the particular attentional operations of the lesioned area, while at the same time considering the contribution of those deficits to other attentional functions.

In one study (Sturm et al., 1997), a computerized rehabilitation program was designed to enhance a specific attentional network. The authors concluded from their findings that vigilance and alertness are the most fundamental aspects of attention and that selective attention and divided attention recruit these functions for their normal operations. A second study that utilized a practice-oriented therapy (attention process therapy) with brain-injured patients showed an overall improvement in performance in comparison with a control group of similar patients (Sohlberg et al., 2000). In some tasks, the group that had relatively high vigilance scores showed better effects as a result of the therapy, in agreement with the Sturm concept.

A third rehabilitation study tested the possible interaction between vigilance and orienting by training patients with right posterior lesions to increase their self-alertness and exploring whether the rehabilitation of self-alertness had an impact on patients' neglect (i.e., orienting deficit; Robertson, Tegnér, Tham, Lo, & Nimmo-Smith, 1995). External warning signals were presented, and patients were instructed to generate a self-alertness signal in response to it. Exogenous alertness, as produced by a loud noise, depends on a thalamo-mesencephalic path and is relatively unimpaired in right parietal patients. After the training procedure was explained, the patient started the task, and at variable intervals the experimenter knocked on the table while at the same time saying "Attend!" in a loud voice. At the next stage in the training, it was the patient who shouted "Attend!" each time the experimenter knocked on the table. Later, the patient would do both the knocking and the vocal command, first loudly, then subvocally, and finally mentally. Patients were encouraged to try this self-alertness method in their everyday lives. This rehabilitation training not only improved patients' self-alertness, but also reduced the extent of their spatial neglect. These samples suggest that rehabilitation that focuses on particular networks is possible; in addition, the attention state training discussed in Chapter 5 may also serve as a means of improving performance of those who have had brain damage. Most efforts at rehabilitation have used practice on a particular network—what we have called attention training. However, it is also possible that a change of state induced by a process such as meditation may serve to produce improvements of attention in patients, as was discussed for normal subjects in Chapter 5.

The availability of imaging as a means of examining brain networks prior to and following rehabilitation should provide new opportunities for research that could fine-tune both behavioral and pharmacological intervention methods. Genetic analysis could also aid in an understanding of who might benefit from particular forms of therapy. These methods and the analysis of attention networks described in this volume could in combination provide significant new approaches to rehabilitation following brain injury.

EDUCATION

Cognitive neuroscience research related to education has most often involved elementary topics such as beginning reading, simple arithmetic, and training attention (Posner & Rothbart, 2007a). We covered much of this work in our book *Educating the Human Brain* and some of it in Chapter 5 of this volume. In this chapter, we concentrate on later education and the ability to acquire expertise in the various domains studied in school.

Multitasking

One important issue that has arisen in recent research is the influence on attention of new media: the increased use of e-mail, computer games, social networking, and so forth. Although direct studies on this topic are few (but see Ophir, Nass, & Wagner, 2009; Lin Lin, 2009, discussed below), many of the principles discussed in this volume can easily be extended to this issue. The influence of training on specific brain networks and brain states makes it seem entirely likely that exposure to new media and dealing with constant interruptions would influence certain brain circuits. Usually discussions of this issue are very one-sided, often citing brain plasticity as a reason why we should be concerned that use of electronic media, for example, is undermining the ability to concentrate. But when it comes to discussions of negative influence, they often consider the brain to be hard-wired and suggest that we are raising a generation that is changed for all time. However, if the brain is plastic, it is as likely that any change induced by the use of media could be changed back by a vacation in the woods with a long intense novel. Indeed, exposure to nature does seem to influence brain states, at least for a time (Tang & Posner, 2009). However, it seems clear that the desire to carry out many tasks at the same time will remain a constant feature of human life.

As we have seen, it is simply not possible for people to carry out multiple tasks that require executive attention at exactly the same time. I experienced a recent reminder of this difficulty. I took my dog and computer to put in my car before backing out of the garage. I did, fortunately, get the dog in the backseat and was sure I had also put the computer there, but in fact I backed the car right over it. Perhaps this was a sign of pending dementia (see last section), but it was also the kind of multitasking error with which we are all familiar. One recent study has compared frequent and less frequent multitaskers and found, rather surprisingly, that the frequent multitaskers were less able to deal with irrelevant information and had frequent interruptions, so they actually performed less well on some multitasking (Ophir et al., 2009). This could mean that the orienting system is drawn to a broader range of sensory cues and this dominates over any training of executive attention that might occur. It shows the importance of distinguishing attention networks in further studies of this type. As pointed out in the commentary on the Ophir et al. article, it may be difficult to extrapolate from interference in a laboratory task (where some information is clearly relevant) to a real-life situation (where what is relevant may not always be so clear and where sensitivity to nonfocal information could itself be an important skill).

Expertise

Much of the study of expertise comes from a strictly behavioral viewpoint, but this approach can be aided by findings from neuroimaging (Posner, in press). The ability to localize areas of brain activity has also revitalized noninvasive electrical and magnetic methods, because it is possible to relate the two and thus to specify the network in terms of both localized brain activity and the time course of that localization. As was pointed out in Chapter 1, this combination has led to the specification of brain networks related to many human activities. Moreover, studies imaging the brain before and after learning have shown that experience can sharpen the efficiency of networks by tuning the neurons at various nodes of the network to increase their ability to carry out localized computation, and as discussed in Chapter 5, experience also improves the connectivity between nodes of the network, which improves overall efficiency.

An aspect of these networks that is somewhat more controversial is the issue of what is localized. The bulk of the evidence supports the idea that computations related to the task being performed are localized, and the overall task is orchestrated through connections between these localized brain areas. This view has been supported in the areas of orienting of attention (Chapter 3) and as an approach to the computations involved in language (Chapter 1; Posner & Raichle, 1994). It is certainly possible that more complex reasoning and memory retrieval processes involve less specific localization (Duncan & Owen, 2000), but these differences may be more due to our weakness in correctly specifying the operations involved than they are to problems with localization.

Common Categories

How does learning change brain networks? As discussed in Chapter 5, it is common for the learning of a task to decrease the amount of brain activation it produces (Durston & Casey, 2006). In some cases, learning reorganizes the brain areas involved; in cases of long continued practice, it can lead to enlarged areas of activation (Kelly & Garavan, 2005). Connectivity of the network can also be enhanced by practice (McNamara, Tegenthoff, Hubert et al., 2007; Tang et al., 2010).

Some categories are common to all members of our species, and we are all experts in tasks that demand their use. An example of such a natural category is human faces, which can influence the infant's behavior at birth. It is believed that perception of faces in the first few months depends primarily on subcortical structures, but by 10 months, there is clear evidence that infants are dealing with faces in a manner quite similar to adults (Johnson, 2004). For adults, faces activate an area of the fusiform gyrus, particularly on the right side, which is called the fusiform face area (Kanwisher, 2000). This brain area is part of the visual system. It probably has a role in organizing the features of the face into a whole so that the face can be recognized through processing by more anterior areas.

A more general function of this area has been discovered, because experts in categories other than faces tend to show activation of this area for the material (e.g., dogs, birds, or automobiles) in which they are expert (Gauthier et al., 1999). This finding demonstrates how the function of a brain area initially associated with recognition of one particular category may, through training, come to be used by other categories (Dehaene & Cohen, 2007).

A similar story underlies the visual word form area. The word form area occupies a part of the fusiform gyrus that is mainly in the left hemisphere; it has been related to chunking visual letters into a unitary whole. Development of the visual word form area is a necessary condition for fluent reading. Just as the face area can be used for other categories, the word form area is not used exclusively for words. There is evidence that visual objects involved in rapid naming tasks can use the same area. These findings suggest the importance of the operations performed on a particular brain area that may be beyond any one kind of information. A particularly striking example of this plasticity is the use of the visual system in the recognition of Braille letters (Pascal-Leone, & Hamilton, 2001). Although the visual system is specialized for visual stimuli, in this case, somatosensory information used in the service of language can utilize visual mechanisms.

The visual word form area is not part of an inborn category; it must be learned with the acquisition of the reading skill. Thus, it represents a kind of learned expertise, but one that is common to many people. Do newly learned categories (such as those involved in many educational topics—history, science, etc.) also involve posterior brain areas? And do these areas operate automatically to structure what is seen, or are they part of a larger problem-solving process? To investigate this issue, it is useful to start with stimuli that have little or no intrinsic meaning to see how they are learned.

Newly Learned Categories

A number of years ago, Steve Keele and I used nonsense patterns of 9 dots, all derived from a single prototype by various distortion rules, in order to explore the learning of new categorical information (Posner & Keele, 1968). Participants learned to sort the patterns into categories represented by four different prototypes. Although the participants were never shown the prototype, they made false alarms in a recognition memory study by reporting falsely that they had seen it before, and prototypes were classified correctly the same proportion of the time as was the case for the learned exemplars. Many behavioral studies showed that this result might be predicted as well by storage of exemplars alone as from models based on representation of the category by the prototype. However, false alarm errors in the recognition memory study suggested the latter view might be correct. As with many behavioral controversies, this one remained unresolved.

Knowlton and Squire (1993) showed that patients whose memory had been impaired by brain lesions were at a great disadvantage in remembering exemplars but dealt very well with the prototype. These studies suggested that extraction of the prototype might not involve the medial temporal brain area found important for explicit storage. This general idea has been confirmed by neuroimaging studies (see Smith, 2008, for a review). Newly learned categories of a variety of visual material seemed to produce activation of posterior visual areas, often more strongly on the right side. It is likely that this is the case for other modalities as well. For example, musical experts shown a picture of a musical instrument activate areas near the primary auditory area (Hoenig et al., 2011)

The idea that new learning builds a sensory representation—highly abstracted, as in the case of the prototype—from the input fits very well with one idea from the work of Chase and Simon (1973) on chess masters. It suggests that the chess master has, within the visual system, a sufficiently abstract representation, so that a newly seen game of chess might be analyzed in terms of already known chess positions. For this to work to produce a memory for the chess master, it would need to work quickly and automatically, without any conscious intent to see the material as related to prior chess games.

One way of examining this issue is to compare conditions when people are asked to explicitly recall an item with conditions in which they can make use of the material, but do not explicitly have to remember it. Studies using word completion presented normal subjects and amnesic patients with a list of words and, after an interval, presented a 3-letter cue either taken from one of the words on the list or not. Subjects were asked to either explicitly recall the word on the list that began with the cue or give the first word associated with the cue (Graf, Squire, & Mandler, 1984; Shimamura, 1986). Normal subjects did much better than amnesiacs under the explicit recall task, but amnesiacs recalled as many words from the list as did the normal subjects when the task was implicit. Moreover, in fMRI studies, implicit use of the primed word seemed to involve a portion of the right posterior cortex (Buckner et al., 1995).

To determine if this activation represented early priming by the stored information, a high-density EEG study was run (Badigaiyan & Posner, 1997). It was found that right posterior electrodes consistent with the fMRI activation differed between primed and unprimed words in the implicit condition during the first 150 milliseconds after input. These data suggested that right posterior activation of information was contacted automatically and rapidly after the input cue. On the other hand, activations in the explicit condition were mostly in hippocampal and frontal areas.

The studies cited here use rather artificial conditions of learning—isolated words or nonsense patterns. One may ask if the same general mechanism is involved with more natural categories learned by experts. Tanaka and Curran (2001) used event-related electrical potentials to show that experts in dogs and birds exhibited differences in brain areas associated with the perception of faces when viewing materials related to their expertise. An early component of the event-related potential (about 170 milliseconds) was associated in the recognition of familiar objects for experts but not for novices. Thus, there appears to be a general neural mechanism by which learning can influence posterior brain areas that can greatly improve the efficiency of handling concepts.

Another feature of the brain circuits related to expertise including faces, word forms, and artificial and natural categories is that, in addition to the posterior area of activation, they also involve frontal areas. In the case of visual words, for example, frontal areas including the left ventral frontal area and the anterior cingulate are active within 150 milliseconds after input, almost as fast as some of the posterior areas (Abdullaev & Posner, 1998). In general, the frontal and posterior areas work together over a long time interval to integrate diverse information related to the problem solution. In the case of generating the use of a noun, which takes about 1,100 milliseconds, the frontal areas are in communication with posterior areas related to semantics at 450 milliseconds (Nikolaev et al., 2001). In general, brain studies have indicated that there is close communication between frontal, posterior, and subcortical areas in generating the solutions to problems, even ones much simpler than those involved in chess.

The study of expertise provides ample evidence that the brain does not start with sensory experience in sensory-specific brain areas and move to final decisions in frontal areas. The brain does not, as Luria believed, produce more and more abstract representations as it moves from posterior to anterior areas. Instead, there is rapid feedback from prefrontal to sensory areas, as well as feed-forward from frontal to posterior areas. Brain studies show that concrete information continues to play a role in concepts and reasoning, as was suggested by Chase and Simon (1973).

COGNITIVE AND SOCIAL NEUROSCIENCE

This section considers a number of issues in social or cognitive neuroscience that have been illuminated and perhaps even solved by brain studies related to attention. It starts with (1) the fundamental question of whether there is a social brain whose modular construction differs from nonsocial networks. Then one of the oldest issues in the field of social psychology is discussed: (2) how much influence do our expectations and higher mental processes have on our perception of the world around us? The next issue is (3) how activation of specific networks (priming) or evocation of different states (insight) influence task performance. Finally, (4) the issue of the primacy of emotion over cognition is discussed. That all of these foundational questions are related to attention suggests how important an understanding of attention is for progress in these fields more generally.

Modularity

There has been a great deal of discussion in the cognitive psychology literature of the concept of modularity. These discussions have often defined modularity in a way that required a system to be unaffected by top-down (e.g., attentional) influences. According to this view, only a very few vertical sensory and motor systems could be modular (Fodor, 1983). However, the evidence that even primary sensory systems can be modulated by attention makes it unlikely that any higher-level brain system will meet the criterion of modularity so defined.

Imaging data provide a rather different perspective on modularity. The material reviewed in this volume suggests that even brain networks that reflect voluntary activity (such as executive attention) may be modular, in the sense that very specific brain areas perform computations reflecting their component operations. This form of modularity does not suggest that these mechanisms will operate in the same way irrespective of strategy or context. Modules in this sense are, like reflexes, never completely separate from other cognitive activity. They are a convenient fiction. However, they do provide a starting place for linking cellular and genetic mechanisms to brain areas and then to cognitive operations and behavior.

Evolutionary psychology researchers have proposed ideas of modularity that challenge the idea of separate attention networks (New, Tooby, & Cosmides, 2007), suggesting that there are no attentional networks but only particular stimuli that have evolved to be selected for behavior. One of these is the category of animals. This research shows that, with other things held constant, animal stimuli are more easily detected than nonanimal stimuli, such as human artifacts (e.g., cars). Although the discussion in the paper of these findings suggests that they are in conflict with the proposed attentional networks discussed in this volume, they are not. There are several ways of accommodating the finding that animals are more visible, if this in fact turns out to be the case. The size or strength of the category of animals, rather than their ability to draw attention, might account for their visibility. Moreover, just as luminance and motion are lower-level features that draw orienting, it could be that being animate is another such feature, very likely for evolutionary reasons. However, none of this would seem to counter the general utility of attentional networks as the sources for improving the perception of objects.

Whether or not there are distinctive brain areas primarily involved in social activity, it seems clear that the same networks of attention discussed in this volume relate to the social world, and that they are modular in the sense that different networks carry out separate attentional functions, but that they are also integrated into a single functioning system.

The New Look in Perception

The so-called "new look in perception" (Bruner, 1957) asked whether expectations taught by our culture can influence the sensory systems that bring information about our world to us. Expectations can occur via attention, or they might reflect the automatic influence of priming from prior learning. The finding discussed earlier in this chapter, that high levels of skill can involve posterior brain systems closely related to sensory-specific cortices, shows that prior learning can influence perception. The skilled person sees the material in a different way that changes perception and performance, even if they are unaware of the influence. The vast difference between hearing words in a foreign language and in our own makes it very clear that the perceptual experience of separate words in our native language is an influence of our prior learning on our perceptions.

The question of how early attention can influence sensory systems arose before there was much discussion of specific brain mechanisms for attention. Many empirical studies were done to determine if attentional changes showed up as alterations in the beta (decision) parameter of a signal detection analysis, or whether they instead involved changes in the d' (sensory) parameter (Hawkins et al., 1990). Although many elegant studies were conducted attempting to clarify this issue, there has been no final resolution, although it seems likely that both parameters can be varied by some experimental conditions (Hawkins et al., 1990). Imaging, however, has clearly shown that even the primary sensory systems can be modified by top-down processes of attention.

The early vs. late question can be resolved into three somewhat interdependent issues:

1. How early in the nervous system can attention influence stimulus input? The results suggest that it can be as early as the primary sensory cortex (Posner & Gilbert, 1999) under some conditions, but more often attention influences later visual areas (Martínez et al., 2001).

2. How quickly after input can attention influence information processing? Again, the cellular and physiological data indicate that it can be about as early as clear evidence of cortical processing can be obtained, although in many situations the influence is not present until 80 to 100 milliseconds after stimulus onset (Martínez, et al., 2001). The timing issue is of particular importance, because activation of a particular

brain area may be either along the input pathway or due to feedback from higher areas.

3. What does early selection mean for the processing of information, both selected and unselected? Here the answer is more complex. One meaning is that certain aspects of complex scenes may be available for conscious report, whereas other aspects will only be available if they succeed in producing reorienting of attention (Rensink et al., 1997). Unattended objects, however, may still be processed to fairly high levels, and the processing itself may summon attention. The depth of cognitive processing of unattended objects and the possibility of attention to higher-level codes suggest that early selection does not have the cognitive consequence originally implied. Selecting one stimulus over others does not mean that unselected items will not produce a reorienting of attention or still influence behavior (McCormick, 1997).

Priming

Priming refers to the influence of one event on the processing of subsequent events. Behavioral studies suggested that reaction time could be improved to a target by the presentation of a stimulus (prime) that shares a part of the same pathway. Priming can occur in either of two ways: In one way, a stimulus activates a pathway automatically and a second stimulus that shares the same pathway is improved in performance (Posner, 1978). These effects can occur even when the prime is presented and masked so that subjects are not able to report its identity. A second way that priming can occur is if a person attends to some feature that will be shared by the target. For example, if people are taught that the word "animal" should be interpreted as a body part, the target "finger" will be primed. The priming is from the subjects' attention to the concept of "body part," not from automatic activation of "finger" by the prime "animal" (Neely, 1976).

Data from imaging studies of priming by input and attention support this distinction by showing very different effects on neural activity in the primed area. If priming occurs automatically by input, the target shows reduced activation of the primed brain area. On the other hand, attending to an area will enhance neural activity and increase the area in which the target is effective (Corbetta et al., 1991).

However, it is not at all clear how the brain brings about similar changes in performance sometimes by reducing and sometimes by increasing the activity of the target. This puzzle remains to be explained by future studies. In this case, the behavioral data seem to be clear, but the mechanism by which the brain makes this possible is much less understood.

The increased attention to highly important stimuli can also be demonstrated on a temporary basis. The ability to draw attention to a category may depend on the temporary strength of that category. Representations of categories in memory change with both priming and repetition (Spitzer et al., 1998). If one has been spending time with this volume, it is likely that ideas about attention may rise to consciousness at times when they are not bidden by any explicit desire to think about the topic. If a comparable portion of time were spent reading about another topic, that topic might instead come to be dominant in thought.

Insight

An issue closely related to priming involves sudden insights into the solution of problems. Often, these insights can come from largely or completely unconscious hints that act like primes. Sensory input or thought may activate a word or concept that unlocks a potential direction for problem solution. Hints can push the problem solver toward a solution, either with or without awareness that the hint may be relevant. If we are unaware of the hint, the problem solution may come as a sudden insight, the origin of which the problem solver has no knowledge.

However, insight may also be influenced by the state of the brain at the time the problem is posed. Recent studies by Kounios and Beeman (2009) and their associates suggest that scalp recordings can provide evidence that a particular brain state fosters the solutions of problems involving insight. (The issue of observing a brain state is discussed in detail in Chapter 2.)

Both specific pathway activity fostered by priming and a general state of the brain can influence insight. This dual process seems somewhat similar to the discussion developed in Chapter 5 that reported specific practice involving attention networks as well as methods that alter brain state, can both be effective in improving attention. Although there is much to be learned concerning insight, we may be at the beginning of learning just how insight can arise from brain mechanisms.

Unconscious Learning

There is a close association between attention and learning. Behavioral studies show that, when close attention is paid to input at the time it occurs, there is a great increase in the likelihood that it will be recalled later. The pathway for this form of learning probably involves feedback from the anterior cingulate to midtemporal areas related to the hippocampus. The hippocampus is involved in distributing and integrating information that, in the long run, is stored in diverse cortical brain areas. The hippocampus is critical for securing long-term storage of information. Although there is much that we do not know about how attention acts to facilitate this process, it seems clear that attention is an important precondition for its occurrence (Squire & Zola-Morgan, 1991).

However, there seems to be equally strong evidence that some forms of long-term storage of information do not rely on specific efforts to store it and do not require the hippocampus. This kind of learning is frequently called implicit; it extends to many domains of learning, from motor skills and sensory information to even verbal information, as was discussed previously in the section on expertise. It seems likely that every neural network has the capability of being strengthened through repetition, even when the activation of the network has not involved executive attention or medial temporal lobe areas usually associated with explicit learning and conscious retrieval. I had one patient with a large tumor that seemed to block his explicit learning of any new material. I showed him a series of 16 pictures. After a 5-minute delay, I asked if he would choose which of two pictures I had previously shown him. He was unaware of having seen the pictures before, but he agreed to guess as a favor to me. I carried out this experiment several times with different lists, which was easy to do because he had no conscious recollection of previous efforts. His performance was 80% correct, showing clearly the kind of priming that we discussed in the last section involving posterior parts of the brain in expertise. Despite repeated efforts, I never was successful in convincing him that he was remembering or in figuring out a way to capitalize on this memory to improve his conscious recall. Much research remains to be done to capitalize on our knowledge of brain states and of consciousness to improve the lives of those with states of diminished awareness.

Emotion and Cognition

The distinguished social psychologist Robert Zajonc developed behavioral experiments that convinced him that emotions did not arise from cognitive processes, but rather frequently preceded our awareness (Zajonc, 1984). What is very clear from brain research is that evaluation of the emotional response to a stimulus is carried out separately from the systems that provide information on its location and identity (Ohman et al., 2007). These experiments show that highly emotional stimuli can activate the amygdala even when they are masked from awareness. Ohman et al. argue that such stimuli draw attention as a result of their automatic activation of the limbic system. This fits with the general argument for unconscious priming of neural networks.

That emotional activation can occur in parallel with cognitive processes should not be surprising because, as we have argued at numerous occasions in this volume, the brain supports many parallel but separate processes. For example, within attention networks, orienting can arise in parallel with alerting. Zajonc also believed that emotional responses were necessarily faster than cognitive ones. That idea seems clearly wrong, as cognitive pathways can be activated with equal rapidity. What **is** correct is that emotional systems can operate in parallel and often more quickly than our awareness of an event, and thus on occasion can serve to guide attention.

The interaction of emotion and cognition is a central topic in both cognitive and social neuroscience. As we have seen in the first part of this chapter, many mental pathologies include a failure by areas of the ventral anterior cingulate to regulate emotion. An understanding of how the mechanisms of attention operate is clearly a critical component in understanding this interaction.

SUMMARY

This chapter has attempted to relate work on attentional networks to topics common in other areas of psychology. We began by dealing with issues of pathology. Attention turns out to be intimately involved in many pathologies and can help to understand methods to remediate some of their symptoms. More broadly attention is intimately related to topics in education including the acquisition of expertise in many domains. Finally we discussed a number of classical issues in psychology that seem to me to have been illuminated by principles developed in the chapters of this volume.

Chapter 7

Concluding Remarks

It is all too common to hear in neuroscience and psychology that attention is a vague concept not amenable to a truly scientific explanation; or that, even if we did have an understanding of the mechanisms of attention, they would do little to illuminate the problems that arise in psychology or social neuroscience. My goal in this volume has been to argue that both of these assertions are false. Although certainly there is much more to be learned, attention is an organ system and thus can be studied network by network, even though—as in all systems—there are interactions among the constituent parts.

As I have argued, attention networks have anatomical and functional independence, but they also interact in many practical situations. Damage to a node of these networks, irrespective of the source, produces distinctive neuropsychological deficits. This principle has been best established with respect to damage to the parietal lobe. Studies have shown that damage to parietal neurons (occurring in stroke, degeneration in Alzheimer's disease, blocking of cholinergic input, lesions of nucleus basalis, temporary damage from transcranial magnetic stimulation, direct injections of scopolamine, or closed head injury) all lead to difficulties in using cues to process targets in the visual field opposite the damage. Normal subjects who have one or two copies of the APOE4 gene, which increases the risk of Alzheimer's disease, have also been shown to have increased difficulty in orienting attention and in adjusting the spatial scale of attention; however, they have no difficulty with maintaining the alert state.

In one sense, the convergence between imaging, lesions, and pharmacology in terms of cognitive effect is obvious. If computations of parietal neurons lead to shifts of visual attention, damage to these neurons should produce difficulties. Yet there has been the notion in neuropsychology that localization is not as important as the cause of the lesion. Moreover, there has also been the argument that imaging does not provide a good account of the computations that can predict the effect of damage (Utall, 2001). Throughout this book, we have seen that imaging results provide clear evidence of the importance of areas of the parietal lobe in orienting of attention, and that damage to these areas—regardless of cause—interferes with aspects of orienting.

In the case of self-regulation, our effort to derive its physical basis (Posner & Rothbart, 2009) depended on the rather surprising relationship between a measure of executive attention derived from the attention network test (ANT) and parental reports of effortful control. This allowed us to discuss how the many nodes of the neural network that carry out resolution of conflict are crucial to self regulation and the important role of anterior cingulate connectivity in influencing many brain areas involved in cognition and emotion. This work has produced a putative brain circuitry underlying self-regulation. The anterior cingulate proved to have an important evolutionary history, including the presence of special cells unique to areas involved in self-regulation in large-brained mammals, notably humans and great apes. Specialization in this area could well be an important part of the unique human ability to delay gratification and to otherwise regulate behavior in the service of long-term goals. This finding provides a renewed opportunity to explore differences between the brains of humans and other primates.

The association of genetic variations with individual differences in the efficiency of networks provides a method for discovery of those genes that serve to build the nodes and connections of the attentional network during development. This link provides a molecular perspective to the physical basis of a complex psychological construct. The ability to find candidate genes related to the attentional network rested on pharmacological findings linking different neuromodulators to the various networks. This opportunity is not present in a majority of the networks shown in Table 1.1. However, other methods, such as the use of full genome scans, the study of brain pathologies, and the use of hints from comparative studies of animals, can be used to provide appropriate candidate genes for other networks.

What illumination will this molecular perspective provide? The conservation of genetic mechanisms along the phylogenetic scale provides a basis for relating developments in human evolution to the more general issues of evolution of our species. As studies of the DRD4 gene suggest, human evolution continues to play a central role in behavior. Evidence for positive selection of alleles of this gene within recent human history has led us to propose the possibility that this and perhaps other alleles may increase the influence of cultural factors, such as parenting, on the child and thus provide for improved reproductive success and enhanced positive selection. This connection between genetic variation and cultural influence shows that the molecular perspective can deepen our understanding of human nature in ways that may be unanticipated. Even though we are very far from a deep understanding of the physical basis of many psychological concepts central to human nature, the tools currently available can foster this effort.

Because attentional networks can influence the operation of other networks, they provide a link between brain mechanisms of attention and what might be called our voluntary behavior. Although this volume does not seek to answer the philosophical question about whether, in principle, all our actions are determined, it does provide critical knowledge of the mechanisms by which we exercise will.

In the preface to this volume I expressed the hope that reading it would help students of social neuroscience in their research. Chapters 5 and 6 summarized how attention may illuminate a wide variety of issues involved in social life. From the socialization of children to the understanding of antisocial behavior (psychopathy) and acquiring expertise, the volume has sought to foster an understanding of the role of attention in human life. Moreover, a tool kit of methods discussed in this volume provides us with the possibility of obtaining further knowledge and thus a firmer basis for the construction of psychology and social neuroscience.

REFERENCES

Abdullaev, Y.G., & Posner, M.I. (1998). Event-related brain potential imaging of semantic encoding during processing single words. *Neuroimage,* 7:1–13.

Ahadi, S.A., Rothbart, M.K., & Ye, R. (1993). Children's temperament in the U.S. and China: Similarities and differences. *European Journal of Personality,* 7:359–378.

Allman, J., Watson, K.K., Tetreault, N.A., & Hakeem, A.Y. (2005). Intuition and autism: A possible role for von Economo neurons. *Trends in Cognitive Science,* 9:367–373.

Allport, A. (1989). Visual Attention in M.I. Posner (ed) Foundations of Cognitive Science. Cambridge MA:MIT Press (Ch. 16, pp. 631–682).

Andersen, R.A. (1989). Visual eye movement functions of the posterior parietal cortex. *Annual Review of Neuroscience,* 12:377–403.

Anderson, S.W., Damasio, H., Tranel, D., & Damasio, A.R. (2000). Long-term sequelae of prefrontal cortex damage acquired in early childhood. *Developmental Neuropsychology,* 18(3):281–296.

Andrews-Hanna, J.R., Snyder, A.Z., Vincent, J.L., Lustig, C., Head, D., Raichle, M.E., & Buckner, R.L. (2007). Disruption of large-scale brain systems in advanced aging. *Neuron,* 56:924–935.

Armstrong, K.M., Chang, M.H., & Moore, T. (2009). Selection and maintenance of spatial information by frontal eye field neurons. *Journal of Neuroscience,* 16:15621–15629.

Aston-Jones, G., & Cohen, J.D. (2005). An integrative theory of locus coeruleus-norepinephrine function: Adaptive gain and optimal performance. *Annual Review of Neuroscience,* 28:403–450.

Attneave, F. (1950). Book Review of D.O. Hebb's *Organization of Behavior. American Journal of Psychology,* 63:633–635.

Auerbach, J.G., Benjamin, J., Faroy, M., Kahana, M., & Levine, J. (2001). The association of the dopamine D4 receptor gene (DRD4) and the serotonin transporter promotor gene (5 HTTL-PR) with temperament in 12-month-old infants. *Journal of Child Psychology and Psychiatry and Allied Disciplines*, **42**:777–783.

Badigaiyan, R., & Posner, M.I. (1997). Time course of cortical activations in implicit and explicit recall. *Journal of Neuroscience*, **17(12)**:4904–4913.

Bakermans-Kranenburg, M.J., & van IJzendoorn, M.H. (2006). Gene-environment interaction of the dopamine D4 receptor (DRD4) and observed maternal insensitivity predicting externalizing behavior in preschoolers. *Developmental Psychobiology*, **48**:406–409.

Bakersmans-Kranenburg, M.J. Van IJzendoorn, M.H., Pijlman, F.T.A., Mesman, J. & Juffer, F. (2008). Experimental evidence for differential susceptibility: dopamine D4 Receptor Polymorphism (DRD4 VNTR) moderates intervention effects on toddlers externalizing behavior in a randomized controlled trial. *Developmental Psychology* **44**:293–300

Baskin-Sommers, A.R., Zeier, J.D., & Newman, J.P. (2009). Self-reported attentional control differentiates the major factors of psychopathy. *Personality and Individual Differences*, **47**:626–630.

Baumeister, R.F., Vohs, K.D., & Tice, D.M. (2007). The strength model of self-control. *Current Directions in Psychological Science*, **16**:351–355.

Beane, M., & Marrocco, R. (2004). Cholinergic and noradrenergic inputs to the posterior parietal cortex modulate the components of exogenous attention. In M.I. Posner, (ed.), *Cognitive Neuroscience of Attention*. New York: Guilford (pp. 313–325).

Beauregard, M., Levesque, J., & Bourgouin, P. (2001). Neural correlates of conscious self-regulation of emotion. *Journal of Neuroscience*, **21**:RC 165.

Beckman, M., Johansen-Berg, H., & Ruschworth, M.F.S. (2009). Connectivity-based parcellation of human cingulate cortex and its relation to functional specialization. *Journal of Neuroscience*, **29**:1175–1190.

Belsky, J., & Pluess, M. (2009). Beyond diathesis stress: Differential susceptibility to environmental stress. *Psychological Bulletin*, **135**:895–908.

Benes, F.M. (1999). Model generation and testing to probe neural circuitry in the cingulate cortex of postmortem schizophrenic brains. *Schizophrenia Bulletin*, **24**:219–229.

Berger, A., Tzur, G., & Posner, M.I. (2006). Infant babies detect arithmetic error., *PNAS*, **103**:12649–12553.

Blair, R.J.R., Morris, J.S., Frith, C.D., Perrett, D.I., & Dolan, R.J. (1999). Dissociable neural responses to facial expression of sadness and anger. *Brain*, **1222**:883–893.

Blasi, G., Mattay, G.S., Bertolino, A., Elvevåg, B., Callicott, J.H., Das, S., Kolachana, B.S., Egan, M.F., Goldberg, T.E., & Weinberger, D.R. (2005).

Effect of Catechol- O-Methyltransferase val[158] met genotype on attentional control. *Journal of Neuroscience,* **25(20)**:5038–5045.

Botvinick, M.M., Braver, T.S., Barch, D.M., Carter, C.S., & Cohen, J.D. (2001). Conflict monitoring and cognitive control. *Psychological Review,* **108**:624–652.

Broadbent, D.E. (1958). *Perception and Communication.* London: Pergamon/ Guilford Press.

Bruner, J. (1957). On perceptual readiness. *Psychological Review,* **64**:123–152.

Buckner, R.L., Petersen, S.E., Ojemann, J.G., Miezin, F.M., Squire, L.R., & Raichle, M.E. (1995). Functional anatomical studies of explicit and implicit memory retrieval tasks. *Journal of Neuroscience,* **15**:5870–5878.

Bullock, T.H., Bennett, M.V.L., Johnston, D., Josephson, R., Marder, E., & Fields, R.D. (2005). The neuron doctrine, redux. *Science,* **310**:791–793.

Bush, G., Frazier, J.A., Rauch, S.L., Seidman, L.J., Whalen, P.J., Jenike, M.A., Rosen, B.R., & Biederman, J. (1999). Anterior cingulate cortex dysfunction in attention-deficit/hyperactivity disorder revealed by fMRI and the counting Stroop. *Biological Psychiatry,* **45**:1542–1552.

Bush, G., Luu, P., & Posner, M.I. (2000). Cognitive and emotional influences in the anterior cingulate cortex. *Trends in Cognitive Science,* **4/6**:215–222.

Buss, A.H., & Plomin, R. (1984). *Temperament: Early developing personality traits.* Hillsdale, NJ: Erlbaum.

Carlson, S.T., & Moses, L.J. (2001). Individual differences in inhibitory control in children's theory of mind. *Child Development,* **72**:1032–1053.

Casey, B.J., Trainor, R., Giedd, J., Vauss, Y., Vaituzis, C.K., Hamburger, S., Kozuch, P., & Rapoport, J.L. (1997a). The role of the anterior cingulate in automatic and controlled processes: A developmental neuroanatomical study. *Developmental Psychobiology,* **3**:61–69.

Casey, B.J., Trainor, R.J., Orendi, J.L., Schubert, A.B., Nystrom. L.E., Giedd, J.N., Castellanos, F.X., Haxby, J.V., Noll, D.C., Cohen, J.D., Forman, S.D., Dahl, R.E., & Rapoport, J.L. (1997b). A developmental functional MRI study of prefrontal activation during performance of a go-no-go task. *Journal of Cognitive Neuroscience,* **9**:835–847.

Chang, F., & Burns, B.M. (2005) Attention in preschoolers: Associations with effortful control and motivation. *Child Development* **76**:247–263.

Chase, W.G., & Simon, H.A. (1973). The mind's eye in chess. In W.G. Chase (ed.), *Visual Information Processing.* New York: Academic Press, 215–281.

Chatty, R., Friedman, J.N., Hilger, N., Saez, E., Schanzenbach, D., & Yagan, D. (2010). How does your kindergarten performance affect your earnings: Evidence from project STAR. On line http://obs.rc.fas.harvard.edu/chetty/STAR_slides.pdf

Checa, P., Rodríguez-Bailón, R., & Rueda, M.R. (2008). Neurocognitive and temperamental systems of self-regulation and early adolescents' social and academic outcomes. *Mind, Brain, and Education,* **2(4)**:177–187.

Cherry, E.C. (1953). Some experiments on the recognition of speech, with one and with two ears. *Journal of the Acoustical Society,* **25**: 975–979.

Chua, H.F., Boland, J.E., & Nisbett, R.E. (2005). Cultural variation in eye movements during scene perception. *PNAS,* **102(35)**:12629–12633.

Clohessy, A.B., Posner, M.I., & Rothbart, M.K. (2001). Development of the functional visual field. *Acta Psychologica,* **106**:51–68.

Cohen, L., Henry, C., Dehaene, S., Martinaud, O., Lehericy, S., Lemer, C., & Ferrieux, S. (2004). The pathophysiology of letter-by-letter reading. *Neuropsychologia,* **42(13)**:1768–1780.

Cohen, R.M., Semple, W.E., Gross, M., Holmbach, H.J., Dowling, S.M., & Nordahl, T.E., (1988). Functional localization of sustained attention. *Neuropsychiatry, Neuropsychology and Behavioral Neurology,* **1**:3–20.

Colcombe, S.J., Kramer, A.F., Erickson, K.I., Scalf, M., Cohen, N.J., Webb, A., Jerome, G.J., Marquez, D.X., & Elavsky, S. (2004). Cardiovascular fitness, cortical plasticity, and aging Source. *PNAS,* **101(9)**:3316–3321.

Conturo, T.E., Lori, N.F., Cull, T.S., Akbudak, E., Snyder, A.Z., Shimony, J.S., McKinstry, R.C., Burton, H., & Raichle, M.E. (1999). Tracking neuronal fiber pathways in the living human brain. *PNAS,* **96(18)**:10422–10427.

Corbetta, M. (1998). Frontoparietal cortical networks for directing attention and the eye to visual locations: Identical, independent, or overlapping neural systems? *PNAS,* **95**:831–838.

Corbetta, M., Miezin, F.M., Dobmeyer, S., Shulman, G.L., & Petersen, S.E. (1991). Selective and divided attention during visual discriminations of shape, color, and speed: Functional anatomy by positron emission tomography. *Journal of Neuroscience,* **11**:2383–2402.

Corbetta, M., Patel, G., & Shulman, G.L. (2008). The reorienting system of the human brain: From environment to theory of mind. *Neuron,* **58**:306–324.

Corbetta, M., & Shulman, G.L. (2002). Control of goal-directed and stimulus-driven attention in the brain. *Nature Neuroscience Reviews,* **3**:201–215.

Crottaz-Herbette, S., & Mennon, V. (2006). Where and when the anterior cingulate cortex modulates attentional response: Combined fMRI and ERP evidence. *Journal of Cognitive Neuroscience,* **18**:766–780.

Curran, T., & Keele, S.W. (1993). Attentional and non-attentional forms of sequence learning. *Journal of Experimental Psychology: Learning, Memory and Cognition,* **19**:189–202.

Dale, A.M., Liu, A.K., Fischi, B.R., Buckner, R., Beliveau, J.W., Lewine, J.D., & Halgren, E. (2000). Dynamic statistical parameter mapping: Combining fMRI and MEG for high resolution cortical activity. *Neuron,* **26**:55–67.

Damasio, A. (1994). *Descartes' Error: Emotion, Reason and the Brain.* New York: G.P. Putnam.

Davidson, M.C., & Marrocco, R.T. (2000). Local infusion of scopolamine into intraparietal cortex slows cover orienting in rhesus monkeys. *Journal of Neurophysiology,* **83**:1536–1549.

Dehaene, S. (1996). The organization of brain activations in number comparison: Event-related potentials and the additive-factors method. *Journal of Cognitive Neuroscience,* **8**:47–68.

Dehaene, S. (1997). *The Number Sense.* Oxford, UK: Oxford University Press.

Dehaene, S., Changeux, J.P., Naccache, L., Sackur, J., & Sergent, C. (2006). Conscious, preconscious, and subliminal processing: A testable taxonomy. *Trends in Cognitive Sciences,* **10**:204–211.

Dehaene, S., & Cohen, L. (2007). Cultural recycling of cortical maps. *Neuron,* 384–398.

Dehaene, S., Posner, M.I., & Tucker, D.M. (1994). Localization of a neural system for error detection and compensation. *Psychological Science,* **5**:303–305.

Dennett, D. (2001). Are we explaining consciousness yet? *Cognition,* **79**:221–237

Derryberry, D., & Reed, M. A. (1994). Temperament and the self-organization of personality. *Development and Psychopathology,* **6**:653–676.

Desimone, R., & Duncan, J. (1995). Neural mechanisms of selective visual attention. *Annual Review of Neuroscience,* **18**:193–222.

Diamond, A. (1991). Neuropsychological insights into the meaning of object concept development. In S. Carey, & R. Gelman (eds.), *The Epigenesis of Mind: Essays on Biology and Cognition* (pp. 67–110). Hillsdale, NJ: Lawrence Erlbaum Associates.

Diamond, A., Barnett, S., Thomas, J., & Munro, S. (2007). Preschool improves cognitive control. *Science,* **30**:1387–1388.

Diamond, A., Briand, L., Fossella, J., & Gehlbach, L. (2004). Genetic and neurochemical modulation of prefrontal cognitive functions in children. *American Journal of Psychiatry,* **161**:125–132.

Ding, Y.C., Chi, H.C., Grady, D.L., Morishima, A., Kidd, J.R., Kidd, K.K., Flodman P, Spence, M.A., Schuck, S., Swanson, J.M., Zhang, Y.-P., & Moyzis, R.K. (2002). Evidence of positive selection acting at the human dopamine receptor D4 gene locus. *PNAS,* **99(1)**:309–314

Dosenbach, N.U.F., Fair, D.A., Miezin, F.M., Cohen, A.L., Wenger, K.K.R., Dosenbach, A.T., Fox, M.D., Snyder, A.Z., Vincent, J.L., Raichle, M.E, Schlaggar, B.L., & Petersen, S.E. (2007). Distinct brain networks for adaptive and stable task control in humans. *PNAS,* **104**:1073–1978.

Drevets, W.C., & Raichle, M.E. (1998). Reciprocal suppression of regional blood flow during emotional versus higher cognitive processes: Implications for interactions between emotion and cognition. *Cognition and Emotion,* **12**:353–285.

Driver, J., Eimer, M., & Macaluso, E. (2004). Neurobiology of human spatial attention: Modulation, generation, and integration. In N. Kanwisher & J. Duncan (eds.), *Attention and Performance XX: Functional Brain Imaging of Visual Cognition* (pp. 267–300).

Dumas, T., Hostick, U., Wu, H., Spaltenstein, J., Ghatak, C., Nguyen, J., & Kentros, C. (2005). Maximizing the anatomical specificity of native neuronal promoters by a subtractive transgenic technique. *Society for Neuroscience Abstracts.*

Duncan, J. (1980). The locus of interference in the perception of simultaneous stimuli. *Psychological Review,* 87:272–300.

Duncan, J. (2010). *The Reason Machine.* New Haven, CT: Yale Univ. Press.

Duncan, J., & Owen, A.M. (2000). Common regions of the human frontal lobe recruited by diverse cognitive demands. *Trends in Neurosciences,* 23:475–483.

Duncan, J., Seitz, R.J., Kolodny, J., Bor, D., Herzog, H., Ahmed, A., Newell, F.N., & Emslie, H. (2000). A neural basis for general intelligence. *Science,* 289:457–460.

Durston, S., & Casey, B.J. (2006). What have we learned about cognitive development from neuroimaging? *Neuropsychologia,* 44:2149–2157.

Early, T.S., Posner, M.I., Reiman, E.M., & Raichle, M.E. (1989). Left striato-pallidal hyperactivity in schizophrenia part II. Phenomenology and thought disorder. *Psychiatric Developments,* 2:85–121.

Eisenberger, N.I., Lieberman, M.D., & Williams, K.D. (2003). Does rejection hurt? An fMRI study of social exclusion. *Science,* 302:290–292.

Ellis, L.K. (2002). Individual differences and adolescent psychosocial development. Unpublished doctoral dissertation, University of Oregon, Eugene.

Ellis, E., Rothbart, M.K., & Posner, M.I. (2004). Individual differences in executive attention predict self-regulation and adolescent psychosocial behaviors. *Annals of New York Academy of Sciences,* 1031: 337–340.

Etkin, A., Egner, T., Peraza, D.M., Kandel, E.R., & Hirsch, J. (2006). Resolving emotional conflict: A role for the rostral anterior cingulate cortex in modulating activity in the amygdala. *Neuron,* 51:871–882.

Everitt, B.J., & Robbins, T.W. (1997). Central cholinergic systems and cognition. *Annual Review of Psychology,* 48:649–684.

Fair, D.A., Cohen, A.L., Power, J.D., Dosenbach, N.U.F., Church, J.A., Meizin, F.M., Schlaggar, B.L., & Petersen, S.E. (2009). Functional brain networks develop from a local to distributed organization. *Public Library of Science,* 5(5):1–13.

Fair, D.A., Dosenbach, N.U.F., Church, J.A., Cohen, A.L., Brahmbhatt, S., Miezin, F.M., et al. (2007). Development of distinct control networks through segregation and integration. *PNAS,* 104(33): 13507–13512.

Fair, D.A., Dosenbach, N.U.F., Petersen, E., & Schlaggar, B.L. (in press). Resting state studies on the development of control systems. In M.I. Posner (ed.) *Cognitive Neuroscience of Attention 2nd.* New York: Guilford.

Fan, J., Bernardi, S. Van Dam, N.T., Anagnostou, E., Gu, X., Martin, L., Park, Y., Liu, X., Kolevzon, A., Soorya, L., Grodberg, D., Hollander, E., & Hof, P.R. (in preparation). Functional deficits of the attentional networks in autism.

Fan, J., Byrne, J., Worden, M.S., Guise, K.G., McCandliss, B.D., Fossella, J., & Posner, M.I. (2007). The relation of brain oscillations to attentional networks. *Journal of Neuroscience,* 27:6197–6206

Fan, J., Flombaum, J.I., McCandliss, B.D., Thomas, K.M., & Posner, M.I (2002). Cognitive and brain mechanisms of conflict. *Neuroimage,* 18:42–57.

Fan, J., Fossella, J.A., Summer T., Wu, Y., & Posner, M.I. (2003). Mapping the genetic variation of executive attention onto brain activity. *PNAS,* 100:7406–7411.

Fan, J., Gu, X., Guise, K.G., Liu, X., Fossella, J., Wang, H., & Posner, M.I. (2009). Testing the behavior interaction and integration of attentional networks. *Brain and Cognition,* 70:209–220.

Fan, J., Kolster, R., Ghajar, J., Suh, M., Knight, R.T., Sarkar, R., & McCandliss, B.D. (2007). Response anticipation and response conflict: An event-related potential and functional magnetic resonance imaging study, *Journal of Neuroscience* 27(9): 2272–2282.

Fan, J., McCandliss, B.D., Fossella, J., Flombaum, J.I., & Posner, M.I. (2005). The activation of attentional networks. *Neuroimage,* 26:471–479.

Fan, J., McCandliss, B.D., Sommer, T., Raz, M., & Posner, M.I. (2002). Testing the efficiency and independence of attentional networks. *Journal of Cognitive Neuroscience,* 3(14):340–347.

Fan, J., Wu, Y., Fossella, J., & Posner, M.I. (2001). Assessing the heritability of attentional networks. *BioMed Central Neuroscience,* 2:14.

Fernandez-Duque, D., & Black, S.E. (2006). Attentional networks in normal aging and Alzheimer's disease. *Neuropsychology,* 20:133–143.

Fink, G.R., Markowitsch, H.J., Reinkemeier, H., Bruckbauer, T., Kessler, J., & Heiss, W.D. (1996). Cerebral representation of one's own past: Neural networks involved in autobiographical memory. *Journal of Neuroscience,* 16(13):4275–4282.

Fischer, T., Langer, R., Diers, K., Brocke, B., & Birmbaumer, N. (2010). Tempero-spatial dynamics of event-related EEG beta activity during the initial contingent negative variation. *Plus One* 5/9 e12514

Fodor, J. (1983). *The modularity of mind: An essay of faculty psychology.* Cambridge, MA: MIT Press.

Fossella, J., Sommer, T., Fan, J., Wu, Y., Swanson, J.M., Pfaff, D.W., & Posner, M.I. (2002). Assessing the molecular genetics of attention networks. *BMC Neuroscience,* 3:14.

Fox, E., Russo, R., Bowles, R.J., & Dutton, K. (2001). Do threatening stimuli draw or hold attention in subclinical anxiety? *Journal of Experimental Psychology— General,* 130:681–700.

Friedrich, F.J., Egly R., Rafal, R.D., & Beck, D. (1998). Spatial attention deficits in humans: A comparison of superior parietal and temporal-parietal junction lesions. *Neuropsychology,* 12(2):193–207.

Friston, K.J., Harrison, L., & Penny, W. (2003). Dynamic causal modeling. *Neuroimage*, **19**(4):1273–1302.

Gailliot, M.T., Baumeister, R.F., DeWall, C.N., Maner, J.K., Plant, E.A., Tice, D.M., Brewer, L.E., & Schmeichel, B.J. (2007). Self-control relies on glucose as a limited energy source: Willpower is more than a metaphor. *Journal of Personality and Social Psychology*, **92**:325–336.

Gao, W., Zhu, H., Giovanello, K.S., Smith, J.K., Shen, D., Gilmore, J.H., & Lin, W. (2009). Evidence on the emergence of the brain's default network from 2 week-old to 2-year old healthy pediatric subjects. *PNAS*, **106**:6790–6795.

Gardner, F. (1983). *Frames of Mind*. New York: Basic Books.

Gauthier, I., Tarr, M.J., Anderson, A.W., Skudlarski, P., & Gore, J.C. (1999). Activation of the middle fusiform gyrus "face area" increases with expertise in recognizing objects. *Neuron*, **34**:161–171.

Gehring, W.J., Gross, B., Coles, M.G.H., Meyer, D.E., & Donchin, E. (1993). A neural system for error detection and compensation. *Psychological Science*, **4**:385–390.

Georgopoulos, A.P., Lurito, J.T., Petrides, M., Schwartz, A.B., & Massey, J.T. (1989). Mental rotation of the neuronal population vector. *Science*, **243**:234–236.

Gerardi-Caulton, G. (2000). Sensitivity to spatial conflict and the development of self-regulation in children 24–36 months of age. *Developmental Science*, **3/4**:397–404.

Goddard, G.V. (1980). Component properties of the memory machine: Hebb revisited. In P.W. Jusczyk & R.M. Klein (eds.), *The Nature of Thought: Essays in Honor of D.O. Hebb*. Hillsdale, NJ: LEA (pp. 231–247).

Gonzalez, C., Fuentes, L.J., Carranza, J.A., & Estevez, A.F. (2001). Temperament and attention in the self-regulation of 7-year-old children. *Personality and Individual Differences*, 30: 931–946.

Graf, P., Squire, L.R., & Mandler, G. (1984). The information that amnesic patents do not forget. *Journal of Experimental Psychology: Learning, Memory and Cognition*, **10**:164–178.

Green, A.E., Munafo, M.R., DeYoung, C.G., Fossella, J.A., Fan, J., & Gray, J.A. (2008). Using genetic data in cognitive neuroscience: From growing pains to genuine insights. *Nature Neuroscience Review*, **9**:710–720.

Green, C.S., & Bavalier, D. (2003). Action video games modify visual selective attention. *Nature*, **423**:434–437.

Griffin, S.A., Case, R., & Siegler, R.S. (1995). Rightstart: Providing the central conceptual prerequisites for first formal learning of arithmetic to students at risk for school failure. In K. McGilly (ed.), *Classroom Lessons: Integrating Cognitive Theory*, Cambridge, MA: MIT Press (pp. 25–50).

Grill-Spector, K. (2004). The functional organization of the visual ventral pathway and its relation to object recognition. In N. Kanwisher & J. Duncan (eds.),

Functional Neuroimaging of Visual Cognition: Attention and Performance XX. Oxford, UK: Oxford University Press, 169–193.

Guttorm, T.K., Leppanen, P.H.T., Poikkeus, A.M., Eklund, K.M., Lyytinen, P., & Lyytinen, H. (2005). Brain event-related potentials (ERPs) measured at birth predict later language development in children with and without familial risk for dyslexia. *Cortex,* **41**(3):291–303.

Haist, R., Adamo, M., Westerfield, M., Courchesne, E., & Townsend, J. (2005). The functional neuroanatomy of spatial attention in autism spectrum disorder. *Developmental Neuropsychology.* **27**:425–458.

Halperin, J.M., & Schulz, K.P. (2006). Revisiting the role of the prefrontal cortex in the pathophysiology of attention-deficit/hyperactivity disorder. *Psychological Bulletin,* **4**:560–581.

Hampton, A.N., & O'Doherty, J.P. (2007). Decoding the neural substrates of reward-related decision making with functional MRI. *PNAS,* **104**(4):1377–1382.

Harman, C., Rothbart, M.K., & Posner, M.I. (1997). Distress and attention interactions in early infancy. *Motivation and Emotion,* **21**:27–43.

Harpending, H. & Cochran, G. (2002). In our genes. *PNAS, 99,* 10–12.

Harter, M.R., & Guido, W. (1980). Attention to pattern orientation-negative cortical potentials, reaction-time, and the selection process. *Electroencephalography and Clinical Neurophysiology,* **49**:461–475.

Hawkins, H.L., Hillyard, S.A., Luck, S.J., Mouloua, M., Downing, C.J., & Woodward, D.P. (1990). Visual attention modulates signal detection. *Journal of Experimental Psychology: Human Perception & Performance,* **16**:802–811.

Haxby, J.V. (2004). Analysis of topographically organized patterns of response in fMRI data: Distributed representation of objects in the ventral temporal cortex. In N. Kanwisher & J. Duncan (eds.), *Functional Neuroimaging of Visual Cognition: Attention and Performance XX.* Oxford, UK: Oxford University Press (pp. 83–97).

Hebb, D.O. (1949). *Organization of Behavior.* New York: Wiley.

Heinze, H.J., Mangun, G.R., Burchert, W., Hinrichs, H., Scholtz, M., Muntel, T.F., Gosel, A., Scherg, M., Johannes, S., Hundeshagen, H., Gazzaniga, M.S., & Hillyard, S.A. (1994). Combined spatial and temporal imaging of brain activity during visual selective attention in humans. *Nature,* **372**:543–546.

Hillyard, S.A., Di Russo, F., & Martinez, A. (2004). The imaging of visual attention. In N. Kanwisher & J. Duncan (eds.), *Functional Neuroimaging of Visual Cognition Attention and Performance XX* (pp. 381–390).

Hobson, J.A. (1999). *Consciousness.* New York: Scientific American Library.

Hoenig, K, Muller, C., Herrnberger, B., Sim, E.J., Spitzer, M., Ehret, G., & Kiefer, M. (2011). Neuroplasticity of semantic representations for musical instruments in professional musicians. *NEUROIMAGE,* **56**(3): 1714–1725.

Hongwanishkul, D., Happaney, K.R., Lee, W.S., & Zelazo, P.D. (2005). Assessment of hot and cool executive function in young children: Age-related changes and individual differences. *Developmental Neuropsychology*, **28(2)**:617–644.

Huang, L.Q., & Pashler, H. (2007). A Boolean map theory of visual attention. *Psychological Review*, **114**:599–631.

Hubel, D., & Wiesel, T.N. (1968). Receptive field and functional architecture of the monkey striate cortex. *Journal of Physiology*, **195**:215–243.

Iwasaki, S. (1993). Spatial attention and two modes of visual consciousness. *Cognition*, **49**:211–233.

Jaeggi, S.M., Buschkuehl, M., Jonides, J., & Perrig, W.J. (2008). Improving fluid intelligence with training on working memory. *PNAS*, **105**:6829–6833.

James, W. (1890). *Principles of Psychology*. New York: Holt.

Johnson, K.A., Robertson, I.H., Barry, E., Mulligan, A. Daibhis, A., Daly, M., Watchorn, A., Gill, M., & Bellgrove, M.A. (2008). Impaired conflict resolution and alerting in children with ADHD: Evidence from the ANT. *Journal of Child Psychology and Psychiatry*, **49**:1339–1347.

Johnson, M.H. (2004). Plasticity and function in brain development: The case of face processing. In J. Duncan & N. Knwisher (eds.), *Attention and Performance XX: Functional Brain Imaging of Visual Cognition*. Oxford, UK: Oxford University Press (pp. 257–266).

Johnson, S.C., Schmitz, T.W., Kawahara-Baccus, T.N., Rowley, H.A., Alexander, A.L., Lee, J.H., & Davidson, R.J. (2005). The cerebral response during subjective choice with and without self-reference. *Journal of Cognitive Neuroscience*, **17(12)**:1897–1906.

Jones, L., Rothbart, M.K., & Posner, M.I. (2003). Development of inhibitory control in preschool children. *Developmental Science*, **6**:498–504.

Kahneman, D. (1973). *Attention and Effort*. Englewood Cliffs, NJ: Prentice Hall.

Kampe, K.K.W., Frith, C.D., & Frith, U. (2003). "Hey John": Signals conveying communicative intention toward the self activate brain regions associated with "mentalizing," regardless of modality. *Journal of Neuroscience*, **23**:5258–5263.

Kanske, P. (2008). Expiring executive attention in emotion: ERP and fMRI evidence. Unpublished dissertation, University of Dresden.

Kanske, P., & Rueda, M.R. (unpublished studies). Alerting and encoding as parallel independent processes.

Kanwisher, N. (2000). Domain specificity in face perception. *Nature Neuroscience*, **3**:759–763.

Kanwisher, N., & Duncan, J. (eds). (2004). Functional neuroimaging of visual cognition. *Attention and Performance XX*. Oxford, UK: Oxford University Press.

Karnath, H-O., Ferber, S., & Himmelbach, M. (2001). Spatial awareness is a function of the temporal not the posterior parietal lobe. *Nature*, **411**:95–953.

REFERENCES

Kastner, S., Pinsk, M.A., De Weerd, P., Desimone, R., & Ungerleider, L.G. (1999). Increased activity in human visual cortex during directed attention in the absence of visual stimulation. *Neuron,* **22**:751–761.

Keehn, B. Lincoln, A.J., Muller, R.A. & Townsend, J. (2010). Attentional networks in children and adolescents with autism spectrum disorder. *Journal of Child Psychology and Psychiatry and Allied Disciplines.* **49**:1296–1303.

Kelly, A.M.C., & Garavan, H. (2005). Human functional neuroimaging of brain changes associated with practice. *Neuroimage,* **15**:1089–1102.

Kerns, K.A., Esso, K., & Thompson, J. (1999). Investigation of a direct intervention for improving attention in young children with ADHD. *Developmental Neuropsychology,* **16**:273–295.

Klein, R. (2008). On the control of attention. *Canadian Journal of Experimental Psychology,* **63**:240–252.

Klingberg, T., Forssberg, H, & Westerberg, H. (2002). Training of working memory in children with ADHD. *Journal of Clinical and Experimental Neuropsychology,* **24**:781–791.

Knowlton, B.J., & Squire, L.H. (1993). The learning of categories: Parallel brain systems for item memory and category knowledge. *Science,* **262**:1747–1749.

Knutson, B., Fong, G.W., Bennett, S.M., Adams, C.M., & Homme, D. (2003). A region of medial prefrontal cortex tracks monetarily rewarding outcomes: Characterization with rapid event-related fMRI. *Neuroimage,* **18(2)**:263–272.

Koch, C., & Tsuchiya, N. (2007). Attention and consciousness: Two distinct brain processes. *Trends in Cognitive Science,* **11**:16–22.

Kochanska, G. (1995). Children's temperament, mothers' discipline, and security of attachment: Multiple pathways to emerging internalization. *Child Development,* **66**:597–615.

Kochanska, G. (1997). Multiple pathways to conscience for children with different temperaments: From toddlerhood to age five. *Developmental Psychology,* **33**:228–240.

Kolb, B. (2003). The impact of the Hebbian learning rule on research in behavioural neuroscience. *Canadian Psychology,* **44**:14–16.

Konrad, K., Neufang, S., Hanisch, C. Fink, G.R. & Herpertz-Dahlmann, (2006). Dysfunctional attentional networks in children with attention deficit/hyperactivity disorder: Evidence from an event-related functional magnetic resonance imaging study. *Biological Psychiatry,* **59**:643–651.

Kosslyn, S. (1980). *Image and Mind.* Cambridge: Cambridge University Press.

Kounios, J., & Beeman, M. (2009). The Aha! Moment: The cognitive neuroscience of insight source. *Current Directions in Psychological Science,* **18**:210–216.

Kuhl, P.K. (2000). A new view of language acquisition. *PNAS,* **100**:11855–11857.

Kuhl, P.K., Stevens, E., Hayashi, A., Deguchi, T., Kiritani, S., & Iverson, P. (2006). Infants show a facilitation effect for native language phonetic perception between 6 and 12 months. *Developmental Science,* **9(2)**:F13-F21.

Kuhl, P.K., Tsao, F.M., & Liu, H.M. (2003). Foreign language experience in infancy: Effects of short-term exposure and social interaction on phonetic learning. *PNAS*, **100**:9096–9191.

LaBerge, D. (1995). *Attentional Processing*. Cambridge, MA: Harvard University Press.

Ladavas, E., Menghini, G., & Umilta, C. (1994). A rehabilitation study of visual neglect. *Cognitive Neuropsychology*, **11**:75–95.

Landry, R., & Bryson, S.E. (2004). Impaired disengagement of attention in young children with autism. *Journal of Child and Adolescent Psychiatry*, **45**:1115–1122.

Larsen, H., van der Zwaluw, C.S., Overbeek, G., Granic, I., Franke, B., & Engels, R.C.M.E. (2010). A variable-number-of-tandem-repeats polymorphism in the dopamine D4 receptor gene affects social adaptation of alcohol use: Investigation of a gene-environment interaction. *Psychological Science*. **21**: 1064–1068

Lashley, K.S. (1929). Brain mechanisms and intelligence A: quantitative study of injuries to the brain. Chicago: University of Chicago Press.

Lassen, N.A., Ingvar, D.H., & Skinhoj, E. (1978). Brain function and blood flow. *Scientific American*, **238**:62–71.

Levitin, D. (2006). *This is Your Brain on Music*. London: Penguin Press

Lin, L. (2009). Breadth-biased versus focused cognitive control in media multitasking Behaviors. *PNAS*, **106**, 37, 15521–22.

Losier, B.J., & Klein, R.M. (2001). A review of evidence on a disengage operation following parietal lobe damage. *Neuroscience and Biobehavioral Reviews*, **25**:1–13.

Luck, S.J., Hillyard, S.A., Mangun, G.R., & Gazzaniga, M.S. (1989). Independent hemispheric attentional systems mediate visual search in split brain patients. *Nature*, **342**:544–545.

Luck, S.J., Hillyard, S.A., Mangun, G.R., & Gazzaniga, M.S. (1994). Independent attentional scanning in the separated hemispheres of split-brain patients. *Journal of Cognitive Neuroscience*, **6**:84–91.

Ludwig, J.C. (2009). Comments on the paper by Michael Posner presented at American Edu. Review Assoc., May 2009.

Luria, A.R. (1973). *The Working Brain*. New York: Basic Books.

Luu, P., Collins, P., & Tucker, D.M. (2000). Mood, personality, and self-monitoring: Negative affect and emotionality in relation to frontal lobe mechanisms of error monitoring. *Journal of Experimental Psychology—General*, **129**:43–60.

Macaluso, E., Frith, C.D., & Driver, J. (2000). Modulation of human visual cortex by cross modal spatial attention. *Science*, **289**:1206–1208.

MacDonald, A.W., Cohen, J.D., Stenger, V.A., & Carter, C.S. (2000). Dissociating the role of the dorsolateral prefrontal and anterior cingulate cortex in cognitive control. *Science*, **288**:1835–1838.

Marrocco, R.T., & Davidson, M.C. (1998). Neurochemistry of attention. In R. Parasuraman (ed.), *The Attentive Brain*. Cambridge, MA: MIT Press (pp. 35–50).

Martínez, A., DiRusso, F., Anllo-Vento, L., Sereno, M., Buxton, R., & Hillyard, S. (2001). Putting spatial attention on the map: Timing and localization of stimulus selection processing striate and extrastriate visual areas. *Vision Research*, 41:1437–1457.

Maruff, P., Currie, J., Hay, D., McArthur-Jackson, C., & Malone, V. (1995). Asymmetries in the covert orienting of visual spatial attention in schizophrenia. *Neuropsychologia*, 31:1205–1223.

Mattay, V.S., & Goldberg, T.E. (2004). Imaging genetic influences in human brain function. *Current Opinion in Neurobiology*, 14(2):239–247.

McCandliss, B.D., Cohen, L., & Dehaene, S. (2003). The visual word form area: Expertise for reading in the fusiform gyrus. *Trends in Cognitive Sciences*, 7 (7):293–299.

McCormick, P.A. (1997). Orienting without awareness. *Journal of Experimental Psychology: Human Perception & Performance*, 23:168–180.

McNamara, A., Tegenthoff, M., Hubert, D., Buchel, C., Binkofski, F., & Ragert, P. (2007). Increased functional connectivity is crucial for learning novel muscle synergies. *Neuroimage*, 35:1211–1218.

Mesulam, M.-M. (1981). A cortical network for directed attention and unilateral neglect. *Annals of Neurology*, 10:309–325.

Milner, P. (2003). The relevance of D.O. Hebb's neural network learning rule to today's psychology. *Canadian Psychology*, 44:5–9.

Molfese, D.L. (2000). Predicting dyslexia at eight years of age using neonatal brain responses. *Brain and Language*, 72:238–245.

Montagna, B., Pestilli, F., & Carrasco, M. (2009). Attention trades off spatial acuity. *Vision Research*, 49:735–745.

Morrison, J.H., & Foote, S.L. (1986). Noradrenergic and serotonergic innervation of cortical, thalamic, and tectal visual structures in old and new world monkeys. *Journal of Comparative Neurology*, 243:117–128.

Moruzzi, G., & Magoun, H.W. (1949). Brain stem reticular formation and activation of the EEG. *EEG & Clinical Neurophysiology*, 1:455–473.

Mountcastle, V.M. (1978). The world around us: Neural command functions for selective attention. *Neuroscience Research Progress Bulletin*, 14(Suppl):1–47.

Nagel, I.E., Chicherio, C., Li, S.C., von Oertzen, T., Sander, T., Villringer, A., Heekeren, H.R., Backman, L., & Lindenberger, U. (2008). Human aging magnifies genetic effects on executive functioning and working memory. *Frontiers in Human Neuroscience*, 2:1–8.

Neely, J.H. (1976). Semantic priming and retrieval from lexical memory: Evidence for facilitatory and inhibitory processes. *Memory & Cognition*, 4:648–654.

Neville, H.J. (in process). Training improves behavior, cognition and neural mechanisms of attention in low SES children.

New, J., Cosmides, L., & Tooby, J. (2007). Category-specific attention for animals reflects ancestral priorities, not expertise. *PNAS*, **104**:16598–16603.

Newell, A. (1990). *Unified Theories of Cognition*. Cambridge, MA: Harvard University Press.

NICHD Early Child Care Research Network. (1993). *The NICHD Study of Early Child Care: A comprehensive longitudinal study of young children's lives*. (ERIC Document Reproduction Service No. ED3530870).

Nikolaev, A.R., Ivanitsky, G.A., Ivanitsky, A.M., Abdullaev, Y.G., & Posner, M.I. (2001). Short-term correlation between frontal and Wernicke's areas in word association. *Neuroscience Letters*, **298**:107–110.

Nimchinsky, E.A., Gilissen, E., Allman, J.M., Perl, D.P., Erwin, J.M., & Hof, P.R. (1999). A neuronal morphologic type unique to humans and great apes. *PNAS*, **96**:5268–5273.

Niogi, S., & McCandliss, B.D. (2009). Individual differences in distinct components of attention are linked to anatomical variations in distinct white matter tracts. *Frontiers in Neuroanatomy*, **3**:21.

O'Reilly, R.C., & Munakata, Y. (2000). *Computational Explorations of Cognitive Neuroscience*, Cambridge, MA: MIT Press.

Ochsner, K.N., Bunge, S.A., Gross, J.J., & Gabrieli, J.D.E. (2002). Rethinking feelings: An fMRI study of the cognitive regulation of emotion. *Journal of Cognitive Neuroscience*, **14**:1215–1229.

Ochsner, K.N., Kossyln, S.M., Cosgrove, G.R., Cassem, E.H., Price, B.H., Nierenberg, A.A., & Rauch, S.L. (2001). Deficits in visual cognition and attention following bilateral anterior cingulotomy. *Neuropsychologia*, **39**:219–230.

Ochsner, K.N., Ludlow, D.H., Knierim, K., Hanelin, J., Ramachandran, T., Glover, G.C., & Mackey, S.C. (2006). Neural correlates of individual differences in pain-related fear and anxiety. *Pain*, **129(1–2)**:69–77.

Ogawa, S., Lee, L.M., Kay, A.R., & Tank, D.W. (1990). Brain magnetic resonance imaging with contrast dependent blood oxygenation. *PNAS*, **87**:9868–9872.

Ohman, A., Carlsson, K., Lundqvist, D., & Ingvar, M. (2007). On the unconscious subcortical origin of human fear. *Physiology and Behavior*, **92**:180–185.

Olesen, P.J., Westerberg, H., & Klingberg, T. (2004). Increased prefrontal and parietal activity after training of working memory. *Nature Neuroscience*, **7(1)**:75–79.

Ophir, E., Nass, C., & Wagner, A.D. (2009) Cognitive control in media multitaskers. *PNAS 106*, **37**:15583–587

Owen, A., & Coleman, M.R. (2007) Functional MRI in disorders of consciousness: advantages and limitation. *Current Opinion in Neurology*, **20**:632–637.

Panksepp, J. (1998). *Affective Neuroscience*. New York: Oxford.

Parasuraman, R., & Greenwood P.M. (2004). Molecular genetics of visual spatial attention and working memory. In M.I. Posner (ed.), *Cognitive Neuroscience of Attention*, New York: Guilford (pp. 245–259).

Parasuraman, R., Greenwood, P.M., Haxby, J.V., & Grady, C.L. (1992). Visuospatial attention in dementia of the Alzheimer type. *Brain*, **115**:711–733.

Parasuraman, R., Greenwood, P.M., Kumar, R., & Fossella, J. (2005). Beyond heritability—Neurotransmitter genes differentially modulate visuospatial attention and working memory. *Psychological Science*, **16**:200–207.

Pardo, J.V., Lee, J.T., Sheikh, S.A., Surerus-Johnson, C., Shah, H., Munch, K.R., Carlis, J.V., Lewis, S.M., Kuskowski, M.A., & Dysken, M.W. (2007). Where the brain grows old: Decline in anterior cingulated and medial prefrontal function with normal aging. *Neuroimage*, **35**:1231–1237.

Pardo, P.J., Knesevich, M.A., Vogler, G.P., Pardo J.V., Towne, B., Cloninger, C.R., & Posner, M.I. (2000). Genetic and state variables of neurocognitive dysfunction in schizophrenia: A twin study. *Schizophrenia Bulletin*, **26**:459–477.

Pardo, J.V. Pardo, P.T., Janer, K.W., & Raichle, M.E. (1990). The anterior cingulate cortex mediates selection in the Stroop attentional conflict paradigm. *PNAS, 87*, 256–259.

Pascal-Leone, A., & Hamilton, R. (2001). The metamodal organization of the brain. Vision: From neurons to cognition. *Progress in Brain Research, 134*:427–445.

Perry, R.J., & Zeki, S. (2000). The neurology of saccades and covert shifts of spatial attention. *Brain*, **123**:2273–2293.

Petersen, S.E., Fox, P.T., Posner, M.I., Mintun, M., & Raichle, M.E. (1987). Positron emission tomographic studies of the cortical anatomy of single word processing. *Nature*, **331**:585–589.

Petersen, S.E. & Posner, M.I. (in press). The attention system of the human brain: twenty years after. Annual Review of Neuroscience.

Posner, M.I. (1975). Psychobiology of attention. In M. Gazzaniga & C. Blakemore (eds.), *Handbook of Psychobiology*. New York: Academic Press (pp. 441–480).

Posner, M.I. (1978). *Chronometric Explorations of Mind*. Hillsdale, NJ: Lawrence Erlbaum Associates.

Posner, M.I. (1980). Orienting of attention. The 7th Sir F.C. Bartlett Lecture. *Quarterly Journal of Experimental Psychology*, **32**:3–25.

Posner, M.I. (1988). Structures and functions of selective attention. In T. Boll & B. Bryant (eds.), *Master Lectures in Clinical Neuropsychology and Brain Function: Research, Measurement, and Practice, American Psychological Association* (pp. 171–202).

Posner, M.I. (1994). Attention: The mechanism of consciousness. *PNAS*, **91**:7398–7402.

Posner, M.I. (2004). The achievements of brain imaging: Past and present. To appear in N. Kanwisher & J. Duncan (eds.), *Attention and Performance XX*. Oxford, UK: Oxford University Press (pp. 505–528).

Posner, M.I. (in press). The expert brain. In J. Stazewski (ed.), *Expertise and skill acquisition: the impact of William G. Chase*. New York: Psychology Press

Posner, M.I., & Cohen, Y. (1984). Components of attention. In H. Bouma & D. Bowhuis eds.), *Attention and Performance X*. Hillsdale, NJ: Lawrence Erlbaum Associates (pp. 531–556).

Posner, M.I., & Fan, J. (2008). Attention as an organ system. In J.R. Pomerantz (ed.), *Topics in Integrative Neuroscience*. New York: Cambridge University Press, Ch.2. (pp. 31–61).

Posner, M.I., & Gilbert, C.D. (1999). Attention and primary visual cortex. *PNAS*, **96/6**:2585–2587.

Posner, M.I., Inhoff, A., Friedrich, F.J., & Cohen, A. (1987). Isolating attentional systems: A cognitive-anatomical analysis. *Psychobiology*, **15**:107–121.

Posner, M.I., & Keele, S.W. (1968). On the genesis of abstract ideas. *Journal of Experimental Psychology*, 77:353–363.

Posner, M.I., & Petersen, S.E. (1990). The attention system of the human brain. *Annual Review of Neuroscience*, **13**:25–42.

Posner, M.I. & Petersen, S.E. (in press). The attention system of the human brain: 20 years after. *Annual Review of Neuroscience*.

Posner, M.I., Petersen, S.E., Fox. P.T. & Raichle, M.E. (1988). Localization of cognitive functions in the human brain. *Science*, **240**:1627–1631.

Posner, M.I., & Raichle, M.E. (1994). *Images of Mind*. New York: Scientific American Books.

Posner, M.I., & Raichle, M.E. (1998). Neuroimaging of cognitive processes. *PNAS*, **95**:763–764.

Posner, M.I., & Rothbart, M.K. (2007a). *Educating the Human Brain*. Washington DC: APA Books.

Posner, M.I., & Rothbart, M.K. (2007b). Attention as a model system for the integration of cognitive science. *Annual Review of Psychology*, **58**:1–23.

Posner, M.I., & Rothbart, M.K. (2009). Toward a physical basis of attention and self-regulation. *Physics of Life Reviews*, **6/2**:103–120

Posner, M.I., & Rothbart, M.K. (2011). Brain states and hypnosis research. *Cognition and Consciousness*. **20** 325–327

Posner, M.I., Rothbart, M.K., & Sheese, B.E. (2007). Attention genes. *Developmental Science*, **10**:24–29.

Posner, M.I., Rothbart, M.K., Sheese, B.E., & Tang, Y. (2007). The anterior cingulate gyrus and the mechanisms of self-regulation. *Journal of Cognitive, Affective and Social Neuroscience*, 7:391–395.

Posner, M.I., Rothbart, M.K., Sheese, B.E., Voelker, P. (in press). Control Networks and Neuromodulators of Early Development. *Developmental Psychology*, doi N:1037/a0025530.

Posner, M.I., Rothbart, M.K., Vizueta, N., Levy, K., Thomas, K.M., & Clarkin, J. (2002). Attentional mechanisms of borderline personality disorder. *PNAS*, **99(25)**:16366–16370.

Posner, M.I., Sheese, B., Odludas, Y., & Tang, Y. (2006). Analyzing and shaping neural networks of attention. *Neural Networks*, **19**:1422–1429.

Price, C.J., & Devlin, J.T. (2003). The myth of the visual word form area. *Neuroimage*, **19**:473–481.

Pylyshyn, Z. (2004). Some puzzling findings in multiple object tracking: Tracking without keeping track of object identities. *Visual Cognition*, **11**:801–822.

Raichle, M.E. (2009). A paradigm shift in functional imaging. *Journal of Neuroscience*, **29**:12729–12734.

Raichle, M.E., Fiez, J.A., Videen, T.O., McCleod, A.M.K., Pardo, J.V., Fox, P.T., & Petersen, S.E. (1994). Practice-related changes in the human brain: Functional anatomy during non-motor learning. *Cerebral Cortex*, **4**:8–26.

Raichle, M.E., MacLeod, A.M., Snyder, A.Z., Powers, W.J., Gusnard, D.A., & Shulman,G.L. (2001). A default mode of brain function. *PNAS*, **98**:676–682.

Rainville, P., Duncan, G.H., Price, D.D., Carrier, B., & Bushnell, M.C. (1997). Pain affect encoded in human anterior cingulate but not somatosensory cortex. *Science*, **277**:968–971.

Rensink, R.A., O'Regan, J.K., & Clark, J.J. (1997). To see or not to see: The need for attention to perceive changes in scenes. *Psychological Science*, **8**:368–373.

Rizzolatti, G., Riggio, L., Dascola, I., & Umilta, C. (1987). Reorienting attention across the horizontal and vertical meridians: Evidence in favor of the premotor theory of attention. *Neuropsychologia*, **25**:31–40.

Robertson, I.H., Tegnér, R., Tham, K., Lo, A., Nimmo-Smith, I. (1995). Sustained attention training for unilateral neglect: Theoretical and rehabilitation implications. *Journal of Clinical and Experimental Neuropsychology*, **17**:416–430.

Robertson, I.H. (1999). Cognitive rehabilitation: Attention and neglect. *Trends in Cognitive Sciences*, **3**:385–393.

Roland, P.E., & Friberg, L. (1985). Localization of cortical areas activation by thinking. *Journal of Neurophysiology*, **53**:1219–1243.

Rosler, F., Heil, M., & Roder, B. (1997). Slow negative brain potentials as reflections of specific modular resources of cognition. *Biological Psychology* 45, 109–141.

Rothbart, M.K. (1989). Temperament and development. In G.A. Kohnstamm, J.E. Bates, & M.K. Rothbart (eds.), *Temperament in Childhood*. Chichester, UK: Wiley (pp. 187–247).

Rothbart, M.K. (2011). *Becoming Who We Are*. New York: Guilford.

Rothbart, M.K., Ahadi, S.A., Hershey, K.L., & Fisher, P. (2001). Investigations of temperament at three to seven years: The Children's Behavior Questionnaire. *Child Development*, **72**:1394–1408.

Rothbart, M.K., & Bates, J.E. (2006). Temperament. In W. Damon, R. Lerner, & N. Eisenberg (eds.), *Handbook of Child Psychology, Social, Emotional, and Personality Development* (6th ed.) (Vol. 3, pp. 99–106). New York: Wiley.

Rothbart, M.K., & Derryberry, D. (1981). Development of individual differences in temperament. In M.E. Lamb & A. L. Brown (eds.), *Advances in Developmental Psychology*. Hillsdale, NJ: Erlbaum (pp. 37–86).

Rothbart, M.K., Ellis, L.K., Rueda, M.R., & Posner, M.I. (2003). Developing mechanisms of effortful control. *Journal of Personality*, **71**:1113–1143.

Rothbart, M.K., Sheese, B.E., Rueda, M.R., & Posner, M.I. (2011). Developing mechanisms of self-regulation in early life. *Emotion Review, 3/2*:207–213

Rueda, M.R., Checa, P., & Santonja, M. (2008). Training executive attention in preschoolers: Lasting effects and transfer to affective self-regulation. Paper presented at the 2008 Annual Meeting of the Cognitive Neuroscience Society.

Rueda, M.R., Fan, J., Halparin, J., Gruber, D., Lercari, L.P., McCandliss B.D., & Posner, M.I. (2004). Development of attention during childhood. *Neuropsychologia, 42*:1029–1040.

Rueda, M.R., Rothbart, M.K., McCandliss, B.D., Saccamanno, L., & Posner, M.I. (2005). Training, maturation and genetic influences on the development of executive attention. *PNAS, 102*:14931–14936.

Rumelhart, D.E., & McClelland, J.L. (1986). *Parallel Distributed Processing*. Cambridge, MA: MIT Press.

Sadaghiani, S., Hesselmann, G., & Kleinschmidt, A. (2009). Distributed and antagonistic contribution of ongoing functions to auditory stimulus detection. *Journal of Neuroscience, 29*:13410–13417

Salthouse, T.A. (2005). Relations between cognitive abilities and measures of executive functioning. *Neuropsychology, 19*:532–545.

Sapir, A., Soroker, N., Berger, A., & Henik, A. (1999). Inhibition of return in spatial attention: Direct evidence of collicular generation. *Nature Neuroscience, 2*:1053–1054.

Savoy, R.L. (2001). History and future directions of human brain mapping and functional neuroimaging. *Acta Psychologica, 107*:9–42.

Schafer, R.J., & Moore, T. (2007). Attention governs action in the primate frontal eye fields. *Neuron, 56*:541–551.

Scherg, M., & Berg, P. (1993). *Brain Electrical Source Anlaysis*. Version 2.0 NeuroScan, Herndon, VA.

Schiff, N.D., Giacino, J.T., Kalmar, K., Victor, J.D., Baker, K., Gerber, M., Fritz, B., Eisenberg, B., Biondi, T., O'Connor, J., Kobylarz, E.J., Farris, S., Machado, A., McCagg, C., Plum, F., Fins, J.J., & Rezai, A.R. (2007). Behavioural improvements with thalamic stimulation after severe traumatic brain injury. *Nature*, **448**:600.

Schiff, N.D., and Fins, J.J. (2007). Disorders of consciousness. Mayo Clinic Proceedings 82, 250–253.

Schmitz, M., Denardin, D., Silva, T.L., Pianca, T., Roman, T., Hutz, M.H., Faraone, S.V., & Rohde, L.A. (2006). Association between alpha-2a-adrenergic receptor gene and ADHD inattentive type. *Biological Psychiatry*, **60**: 1028–1033.

Sejnowski, T.J. (2003). The once and future Hebb synapse. *Canadian Psychology,* **44**:17–20.

Shaw, T.H., Warm, J.S., Finomore, V., Tripp, L., Matthews, G., Weiler, E., & Parasuraman, R. (2009). Effects of sensory modality on cerebral blood flow velocity during vigilance. *Neuroscience Letters,* **461**:207–211.

Shannon, B.J., Raichle, M.E., Snyder, A.Z., Fair, D.A., Mills, K.L., Zhanaag, D., Bache, K., Calhoun, V.D. Nigg, J.T., Nagel, B.J., Stevens, A.A., & Kiehl, K.A. (2011). Premotor functional connectivity predict impulsivity in juvenile offenders. *PNAS* **108**:11241–11245.

Sheese, B.E., Rothbart, M.K., Posner, M.I., White, L.K., & Fraundorf, S.H. (2008). Executive attention and self-regulation in infancy. *Infant Behavior and Development,* **31**:501–510.

Shelton, A.L., & Gabrieli, J.D.E. (2002). Neural correlates of encoding space from route and survey perspectives. *Journal of Neuroscience,* **22(7)**:2711–2717.

Shimamura, A.P. (1986). Priming effect in amnesia—evidence for a dissociable memory function. *Quarterly Journal of Experimental Psychology,* **38**:619–644.

Shulman, G.L., Astafiev, S.V., Franke, D., Pope, D.L.W., Snyder, A.Z., McAvoy, M.P., & Corbett, M. (2009). Interaction of stimulus-driven reorienting and expectation in ventral and dorsal frontoparietal and basal ganglia-cortical networks. *Journal of Neuroscience,* **29**:4392–4407.

Shulman, G.L., Remington, R.W., & McClean, J.P. (1979). Moving attention through space. *Journal of Experimental Psychology: Human Perception and Performance,* **5**:522–526.

Silbersweig, D., Clarkin, J.F., Goldstein, M., Kernberg, O.F., Tuescher, O., Levy, K.N., Brendel, G., Pan, H., Beutel, M., Pavony, M.E., Epstein, J., Lenzenweger, M.F., Thomas, K.M., Posner, M.I., & Stern, E. (2007). Failure of frontolimbic inhibitory function in the context of negative emotion in borderline personality disorder. *American Journal of Psychiatry,* **164**:1832–1841.

Smith, E.E., Jonides, J., Marshuetz, G., & Koeppe, R.A. (1998). Components of verbal working memory. *PNAS,* **95**:876–882.

Sohlberg, M.M., McLaughlin, K.A., Pavese, A., Heidrich, A., & Posner, M.I. (2000). Evaluation of attention process therapy training in persons with acquired brain injury. *Journal of Clinical and Experimental Neuropsychology,* **22**:656–676.

Sokolov, E.N. (1958). *Perception and the conditioned reflex.* New York: McMillan.

Spitzer, M., Kischka, U., Guckel, F., Bellemann, M.E., Kammer, T., Seyyedi, S., Weisbrod, M., Schwartz, A., & Brix, G. (1998). Functional magnetic resonance imaging of category-specific cortical activation, evidence for semantic maps. *Cognitive Brain Research,* **6(4)**:309–319.

Squire, L.R., & Zola-Morgan, S. (1991). The medial temporal lobe memory system. *Science,* **253**:1380–1386.

Stevenson, J., Langley, K., Pay, H., Payton, A, Worthington, J, Ollier, W, & Thapar, A. (2005). Attention deficit hyperactivity disorder with reading disabilities: Preliminary genetic findings on the involvement of the ADRA2A gene. *Journal of Child Psychology and Psychiatry,* **46**:1081–1088.

Stewart, C., Burke, S., & Marrocco, R. (2001). Cholinergic modulation of covert attention in the rat. *Psychopharmocology,* **155(2)**:210–218.

Sturm, W., Thimm, A., Kuest, J., Karbe, H. & Fink, G.R. (2006). Alertness-training in neglect: Behavioral and imaging results. *Restorative Neurology and Neuroscience,* **24**:371–384.

Sturm, W., & Willmes, K. (2001). On the functional neuroanatomy of intrinsic and phasic alertness. *Neuroimage,* **14**:S76-S84.

Sturm, W., Willmes, K., Orgass, B., & Hartje, W. (1997). Do specific attention deficits need specific training? *Neuropsychological Rehabilitation,* **7(2)**:81–103.

Sutton, S., Nraren, M., Zubin, J., & John, E.R. (1965). Evoked potential correlates of stimulus uncertainty. *Science,* **150**:1187–1188.

Swanson, J.M., Floodman, P., Kennedy, J.M., Spence, A.M., Moyzes, M., Schruck, S., Murias, M., Moriarty, J, Barr, C., Smith, M., & Posner, M.I. (2000). Dopamine genes and ADHD. *Neuroscience & Biobehavioral Reviews,* **24**:1:21–25.

Swanson, J., Oosterlaan J., Murias, M., Schuck, S., Flodman, P., Spence, M.A., Wasdell M., Ding, Y., Chi, H., Smith, M., Mann, M., Carlson, C., Kennedy, M.J., Sergeant, J., Leung, P., Zhang, Y., Sadeh, A., Chen, C., Moyzis, R., Posner, M.I. (2000). ADHD children with 7-repeat allele of the DRD4 gene have extreme behavior but normal performance on critical neuropsychological tests of attention. *PNAS,* **97**:4754–4759.

Swanson, J.M., Posner, M.I., Potkin, S., Bonforte, S., Youpa, D., Cantwell, D. & Crinella, F. (1991). Activating tasks for the study of visual-spatial attention in ADHD children: A cognitive anatomical approach. *Journal of Child Neurology,* **6**: S119–S127.

Takarae, Y., Schmidt, L., Tassone, F., & Simon, T.J. (2009). Catechol-O-methyltransferase polymorphism modulates cognitive control in children with chromosome 22q11.2 deletion syndrome. *Cognitive Affective and Behavioral Neuroscience,* **9(1)**: 83–90.

Tanaka, J.W., & Curran T. (2001). A neural basis for expert object recognition. *Psychological Science,* **12**:43–47.

Tang, Y., & Posner, M.I. (2009). Attention training and attention state training. *Trends in Cognitive Science,* **13**:222–227.

Tang, Y.Y., Ma, Y., Wang, J., Fan, Y., Feng, S., Lu, Q., Yu, Q., Sui, D., Rothbart, M.K. Fan, M., & Posner, M.I. (2007). Short-term meditation training improves attention and self-regulation. *PNAS,* **104**:17152–17156.

Tang, Y.Y., Ma, Y., Fan, Y., Feng, H., Wang, J., Feng, S., Lu, Q., Hu, B., Lin, Y., Li, J., Zhang, Y., Wang, Y., Zhou, L., & Fan, M. (2009). Central and autonomic nervous system interaction is altered by short-term meditation. *PNAS.* **106(22)**: 8865–70.

Tang, Y., Lu, Q., Geng, X., Stein, E.A., Yang, Y., & Posner, M.I. (2010). Short term mental training induces white-matter changes in the anterior cingulated. *PNAS* **107**:16649–16652.

Thomas, A., & Chess, S. (1977). *Temperament and Development.* New York: Brunner/Mazel.

Thomas, A., Chess, S., Birch, H.G., Hertzig, M.E., & Korn, S. (1963). *Behavioral Individuality in Early Childhood.* New York: New York University Press.

Thompson, K.G., Biscoe, K.L., & Sato, T.R. (2005). Neuronal basis of covert spatial attention in the frontal eye fields. *Journal of Neuroscience,* **25**:9479–9487.

Tough, P. (2008). *Whatever It Takes.* Boston: Houghton Mifflin.

Townsend, J., & Courchesne, E. (1994). Parietal damage and the narrow spotlight of spatial attention. *Journal of Cognitive Neuroscience,* **6**:220–232.

Townsend, J., Keene, B., & Westerfield, M. (in press). Abstraction of mind: attention in autism. In M.I. Posner (ed). *Cognitive Neuroscience of Attention 2nd Ed.* New York: Guilford.

Treisman, A.M., & Gelade, G. (1980). Feature integration theory of attention. *Cognitive Psychology,* **12**:97–136.

Tucker, D.M., Luu, P., Frishkoff, G., Quiring, J., & Poulsen, C. (2003). Frontolimbic response to negative feedback in clinical depression. *Journal of Abnormal Psychology,* **112**:667–678.

Turken, A.U., & Swick, D. (1999). Response selection in the human anterior cingulate cortex. *Nature Neurosceince,* **2(10)**:920–924.

Ungerleider, L.G., Courtney, S.M., & Haxby, H.V. (1998). A neural system for human visual working memory. *PNAS,* **95**:883–890.

Utall, W.R. (2001). *The New Phrenology.* Cambridge, MA: MIT Press.

van IJzendoorn, M.H., & Bakermans-Kranenburg, M.J. (2006). DRD4 7-repeat polymorphism moderates the association between maternal unresolved loss or trauma and infant disorganization. *Attachment and Human Development,* **8**:291–307.

van Veen, V., & C.S. Carter. (2002). The timing of action-monitoring processes in the anterior cingulate cortex. *Journal of Cognitive Neuroscience,* **14**:593–602.

Van Voorhis, S.T., & Hilyard, S.A. (1977). Visual evoked potential and selective attention to points in space. *Perception and Psychophysiology,* **1**:54–62.

Venter, J.C., Adams, M.D., Myers, E.W., Li, P.W., Mural, R.J., Sutton, et al. (2001). The sequence of the human genome. *Science,* **291**:1304–1335.

Vincent, J.L., Patel, G.H., Fox, M.D., Snyder, A.Z., Baker, J.T., Van Essen, D.C., Zempel, J.M., Snyder, L.H., Corbetta, M., & Raichle, M.E. (2007). Intrinsic functional architecture in the anaesthetized monkey brain. *Nature,* **447**:83–84.

Voelker, P., Sheese, B.E., Rothbart, M.K., & Posner, M.I. (2009). Variations in COMT gene interact with parenting to influence attention in early development. *Neuroscience,* **164(1)**:121–130.

Volpe, B.T., LeDoux, J.E., & Gazzaniga, M.S. (1979). Information processing of visual stimuli in an extinguished visual field. *Nature,* **282**:1947–1952.

Voytko, M.L., Olton, D.S., Richardson, R.T., Gorman, L.K., Tobin, J.R., & Price, D.L., (1994). Basal forebrain lesions in monkeys disrupt attention but not learning and memory. *Journal of Neuroscience,* **14(1)**:167–186.

Vygotsky, L.S. (1934). *Thought and Speech.* Moscow: Sotsekgiz.

Walter, W.G., Cooper, R., Aldridge, V.J., McCallum, W.C., & Winter, A.L. (1964). Contingent negative variation: An electrical sigh of sensorimotor association and expectancy in the human brain. *Nature,* **203**:380–384.

Wang, B., Wang, Y.F., Zhou, R.L., Li, J., Qian, Q.J., Yang, L., Guan, LL., & Faraone, S.V., (2006a). Possible association of the alpha-2 adrenergic receptor gene (ADRA2A) with symptoms of attention-deficit/hyperactivity disorder. *American Journal of Medical Genetics Part B-Neuropsychiatric Genetics,* 141B.

Wang, E.T., Ding, Y.-C., Flodman, P., Kidd, J.R., Kidd, K.K., Grady, D.L., & Moyzis, R.K. (2004). The genetic architecture of selection at the human dopamine receptor D4 (DRD4) gene locus. *The American Journal of Human Genetics,* **74**:931–944.

Wang, E.T., Kodama, G., Baldi, P., & Moyzis, R.K. (2006b). CH4 Global landscape of recent inferred Darwinan selection for Homo sapiens. *PNAS,* **103**:135–140.

Wang, H., & Fan, J. (2007). Human attentional networks: A connectionist model. *Journal of Cognitive Neuroscience,* **19**:1678–1689.

Wang, K.J., Fan, J., Dong, Y., Wang, C., Lee, T.M.C., & Posner, M.I., (2005). Selective impairment of attentional networks of orienting and executive control in schizophrenia. *Schizophrenia Research,* **78**:235–241.

Whittle, S. (2007). The neurobiological correlates of temperament in early adolescents. Unpublished doctoral dissertation, University of Melbourne, Australia.

Wojciulik, E., Kanwisher, N., & Driver, J. (1998). Covert visual attention modulates face-specific activity in the human fusiform gyrus: fMRI study. *Journal of Neurophysiology,* **79(3)**:1574–1578.

Womelsdorf, T., Fries, P., Mitra, P.P., & Desimone, R. (2006). Gamma-band synchronization in visual cortex predicts speed of change detection. *Nature,* **439**:733–736.

Womelsdorf, T., Schoffelen, J.M., Oostenveld, R., Singer, W., Desimone, R., Engel, A.K., & Fries, P. (2007). Modulation of neuronal interactions through neuronal synchronization, *Science,* **316**:1609–1612.

Wright, R.D., & Ward, L.M. (2008). *Orienting of Attention.* Oxford, UK: Oxford University Press.

Wurtz, R.H., Goldberg, E., & Robinson, D.L. (1980). Behavioral modulation of visual responses in monkey: Stimulus selection for attention and movement. *Progress in Psychobiology and Physiological Psychology,* **9**:43–83.

Wynn, K. (1992). Addition and subtraction by human infants. *Nature,* **358**:749–750.

Zajonc, R.B. (1984). On the primacy of affect. *American Psychologist,* **39**:117–123.

Zeier, J.D., Maxwell, J.S., & Newman, J.P. (2009). Attention moderates the processing of inhibitory information in primary psychopathy. *Journal of Abnormal Psychology,* **118**:554–563.

AUTHOR INDEX

SUBJECT INDEX

ACT-R, 23–24. *See also* attention, ANT
alertness, 28–47
   and ADHD, 43–44, 45–46, 128–30
   and alterations produced by brain damage, 29
   and errors, 39, 40, 103, 105, 116
   and learning disabilities, 44
   and RT (reaction time), 22, 29, 38–43, 49, 51, 53, 54, 67, 70, 87, 92, 104 Table 5.1, 150
      CNV (contingent negative variation), 28–29, 33, 36, 37
      subtraction and, 23, 38, 41, 88
   arousal, 28–46, 83, 102
      cholinergic, 28
      dopaminergic, 28
      noradrenergic, 28
   development of, 32, 35, 40–43
   errors, monitoring and correction of, 39, 40, 103, 105, 116
   genes and, 17, 43–44
   neglect, 15, 44, 45, 56, 57, 62, 70, 137
   phasic, 19, 23, 35–40, 45, 47
   restoration of after brain injury, 44–45
   tonic, 20, 23, 33–35, 42, 43, 45, 46, 47, 128
   See also ADHD; brain, thalamus
AD (Alzheimer's disease), 44, 56, 68, 124, 129, 156
   and APOE gene, 68–69, 71, 156–57

ADHD. *See* attention
ASD (autistic spectrum disorder), 130
ANT. *See* attention
arithmetic, 9 Table 1.1
   brain areas involved in doing mental, 58, 122
   learning, 13, 138
attention
   ADHD (Attention Deficit Hyperactivity Disorder) and, 44, 45, 109–12, 120, 128–30, 136
      alerting network behavioral deficit, 46
      executive network behavioral deficit, 45–46
      sleep problems and, 46, 128–29
   ANT (attention network test) and, 22–26, 33, 34, 35, 40, 43, 44, 45, 47, 87, 88, 93, 94, 122, 128, 130, 134, 157
      and ADHD, 45–46, 129
      and Alzheimer's disease, 44, 129
      and ASD, 130
      and borderline personalities, 133
      and child development, 93
      and dopamine, 25
      and schizophrenia, 134
   conflict resolution and, 41, 42–43, 73, 74, 76, 119 (*see also* Stroop effect)